SEXUAL
PREDATOR

Sexual Predator:
How to Identify Registered and Unregistered Sex Offenders
(c) 1999 by Robert Scott

Published by:
Crime Time Publishing Co.
289 S. Robertson Blvd., PMB 224
Beverly Hills, CA 90211

www.crimetime.com

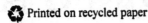 Printed on recycled paper

Printed in the United States of America
10 9 8 7 6 5 4 3 2 1
First edition

Scott, Robert
Sexual predator: how to identify registered
and unregistered sex offenders/by Robert Scott
— 1st ed.
p. cm.
LCCN: 99-095695
ISBN: 0-9652369-3-5
1. Sex offenders—Unites States—Registers.
2. Criminal registers—United States—States.
3. United States. Megan's Law. 4. Investigations—
Handbooks, manuals, etc. 5. Sex crimes—United
States—Prevention. I. Title.

HV6592.S36 1999   364.15'3
                    QB199-1303

DISCLAIMER

This book is for informational purposes only and any reliance upon the information contained herein is at the sole risk of its user.

Although every reasonable effort has been made to present accurate and complete information in this book, errors may be contained in the information presented. In addition, availabilty of public records as described in this book may have changed since publication date. Information contained in this book should be verified with the appropriate government agencies. No warranties, either expressed or implied, are made by the author, publisher or distributors of this book.

SEXUAL
PREDATOR

How to Identify Registered and Unregistered Sex Offenders

by
Robert Scott, P.I.

CRIME TIME
PUBLISHING CO.

CONTENTS

CONTENTS

More

CONTENTS

HOW TO USE

and NOT use this book

How to Use and NOT Use This Book

At the very moment you are reading this sentence, a sexual predator is seeking out his next victim and preparing to strike. Adrenaline is surging into his bloodstream. His darkest animal impulses are overwhelming more rational thought processes. The crime may occur moments from now, or it may occur days from now, depending on the patience of the predator and the wariness of the prey. But regardless, the predator will strike and another innocent person will be victimized.

In the case of serial child molesters, the number of victims attributable to one predator can be staggering — in the hundreds. They use cunning, manipulation, affection and blackmail to achieve their objectives. In the case of rapists who prey on adults, the number of victims will typically be less — but the devastation experienced will be just as great. Rather than using skillful manipulation, these crimes will rely on violence or the threat of violence. Studies have already shown that with or without sex offender registration and community notification laws, many of these offenders will re-offend — some over and over again.

What good then is this book, or any precaution, such as checking a sex offender registry, if these sexual predators will strike regardless? The answer to this is simple: *Yes, they may strike again — but who their next victim will be will be determined by the precautions that you take today. Those who take precautions as described in this book will minimize the chance that they, their family or their neighbors will be victimized. Conversely, those who forsake precautions increase their chances of becoming a victim.* Let's look at two recent true stories which clearly illustrate this:

In California, a convicted sex offender was paroled from state prison after serving ten years for rape, sodomy, assault and burglary. Soon after moving to a small town on the state's central coast, his identity was learned by local residents using Megan's Law. Megan's Law, which you will shortly learn how to use, is the law that allows notification to the community when a sex offender moves into the area. Although no overt harassment occurred, neighbors circulated letters warning each other of the registered sex offender's presence. The offender chose to move on to a new town where he might be able to live out from under the shadow of his criminal past. Although he re-registered at his new address as required by law, local residents in his new

2

town *failed* to check the state's sex offender registry. A short time later, a coed disappeared without a trace from a nearby campus. Then a second coed disappeared. Police investigators ultimately traced the missing women back to the rented property of the registered sex offender where their corpses were found buried. Shortly after his arrest, the murderer expressed his gratitude at being stopped and, according to a local newspaper, said, "If I'm not a monster, then what am I?"

Now, in fairness to the victims in this case, I'm not suggesting that their failure to study and memorize the faces of locally registered sex offenders caused their demise. In fact, the offender who was charged with their murder traveled out of his immediate town to the local campus some 15 miles away. However, what I am suggesting is indisputable: The residents of the first town where this predator lived were vigilant. They used Megan's Law and learned that a paroled rapist was living in their midst. As a result, the predator moved on and they were not victimized. Their vigilance didn't affect whether or not the offender would re-offend — rather, just *where* he would strike and *who* would be his next victim.

Here's another recent true story, from a small city in New England. A man used Megan's Law to check his state's sex offender registry and learned that a registered sex offender had rented an apartment overlooking the playground of a local elementary school. When the man brought this to the attention of local police, it was determined that the offender was paroled on child molestation charges and was in violation of a condition of his parole that he stay at least 1,000 feet away from all schools. The sex offender was returned to prison — and children who might have been victimized were not.

Now, will this offender strike again when he is ultimately re-released from prison? Based on his close proximity to the elementary school described above, the answer, in all likelihood, is yes. However, through the vigilance of a single citizen and his lawful usage of Megan's Law, children who might have been victimized were not.

Today there are over *one-half million* convicted sex offenders who have been released from jail or prison and are living in our communities. These persons have committed various sex-related crimes including child molestation, rape and other sexual assaults.

Are all of these ex-convicts looking to prey on our young or on our women? Certainly not. Among them are those who have successfully rehabilitated and now lead normal, productive lives. They raise families. They pay taxes. They go to church.

Unfortunately, also in this group is the habitual, predatory repeat offender who is perpetually searching for his latest victim. This particularly dangerous brand of sex offender is referred to by experts as a "Sexual Predator".

What is society to do about sex offenders and sexual predators? Some would argue a "One Strike" approach where one offense is sufficient to warrant maximum punishment along the lines of execution, castration or permanent incarceration. Others may argue along a more moderate tack, believing that it is important to protect the right of the one-time offender to rehabilitate and rejoin society after due punishment. Persons supporting this position often point out, correctly, that many sex offenders were victims of sexual abuse themselves at some point in their life.

Still others believe that the ultimate answer may lie in technology — the use of drugs and hormones ("chemical castration"), or non-removable radio transmitter anklets that track the whereabouts of the offender through satellite technology.

But for the person who just wants to be safe and have peace of mind, these questions may be little more than intellectual badminton. This person, probably you, is really in search of an answer that is more immediate: What can I do to protect my family, my community and myself *today*? The answer couldn't be more uncomplicated: *Learn to identify sex offenders who might be dangerous, and be watchful so that they are not given the opportunity to victimize you, your family or your community.*

How to Use This Book

Did you know that convicted sex offenders are identifiable through one of several different categories of government records? These are actual lists of names of persons who have been convicted of rape, child molestation and other crimes. These lists include sex offender registries, statewide criminal record repositories and other government records. They are often available to the public — for those who know where to look.

With this book you have a step-by-step guide that will be your first line of defense against sexual predators by teaching you how to identify registered and unregistered sex offenders. You'll learn to conduct a name search, which is how to check on the background of a particular individual. You'll also learn how to conduct a community search, which allows you to learn if there are any registered sex offenders living in a specific geographic area.

You may have already noticed that I make the distinction between two types of sex offenders — *registered* and *unregistered*. This is because some states have very narrow requirements as to who qualifies as a sex offender requiring registration. Typically, these narrow requirements arise out of constitutional grounds, not weak-minded politicians. In many states, retroactively applying sex offender registration laws to persons convicted prior to enactment of the law is not constitutional.

For example, in New Mexico, only sex offenders whose crimes were committed after July 1, 1999 can be found in the state's sex offender registry. Obviously, this will not give many people a lot of peace of mind about Megan's Law there. A child molester or other sex offender could have several past convictions — but if none were after July 1, 1999, he'd come up "clean" in a check of the state's sex offender registry!

Unfortunately, New Mexico is not the only state whose version of Megan's Law falls far short of truly protecting the public. In fact, there are weaknesses in how Megan's Law is applied in many states. Throughout this book, these shortcomings will be brought to

7

your attention so that you won't over rely on incomplete information. In these cases, you'll want to go one step further and check for *unregistered* sex offenders by using statewide criminal histories and other records. In short, these provide back doors to the same information that is blocked by inadequate versions of Megan's Law.

Before moving on, I should make one thing crystal clear: Although I point out shortcomings in Megan's Law as it exists in many states throughout this book, my intention is not to be overly critical. In fact, in many places Megan's Law is being put to effective use and is offering real protection to the public. I am convinced that as a result of this law, countless potential victims — child and adult — have been spared the trauma of victimization by these sexual predators.

How To NOT Use This Book

This book urges you to do several things to protect yourself and your family. One thing it does *not* suggest is you take the law into your own hands by conducting any unlawful act against a sex offender. There are several important reasons why harassment should *never* be directed at one of these offenders:

• *Harassment, vigilantism or other illegal actions could*

drive registered sex offenders underground as well as create a public backlash leading to the weakening or abolition of Megan's Law.

• *You screwed up! You mistakenly identified an innocent person as a registered sex offender...and to compound your misstep, you harassed this innocent person.*

• *The sex offender may have rehabilitated long ago and now leads an exemplary life. He or she made a one-time mistake and has corrected his or her life.*

This book does *not* provide advice as to what should be done when you learn that a neighbor, a tenant, an employee or other person is a previously convicted sex offender. Every situation is unique and should be handled as such. *If you believe that your own safety or that of others is in imminent danger, contact your local police department for assistance.*

In summary, your ability to responsibly put to use the information contained in this book will allow you, your family and your community to lead a safer life with more peace of mind. On the other hand, misusing this information could lead to a host of legal and moral implications. In short, my message to you is *practice vigilance, not vigilantism.*

How to Identify Registered Sex Offenders

How to Identify Registered Sex Offenders

July 29th, 1994 was hot in Hamilton Township, New Jersey and there was no breeze to speak of. By quarter-to-seven, dinner was over and the day's heat still hung in the air. Indoors was the last place seven-year-old Megan Kanka wanted to be. When she left her house in search of a playmate, a series of events were about to unfold that would culminate in a national debate over how society should protect itself from convicted sex offenders who had served their time and were released back into society.

Just out of first grade, Megan was an easy target for 33-year-old Jesse Timmendequas who lived across the street in this pleasant, tree-dotted neighborhood of middle-class homes. Timmendequas was a parks worker for a nearby town who never attracted much attention to himself. In short, he was the type of person who could be overlooked in a crowd of one.

Timmendequas shared his house with two other

single men and had been secretly keeping an eye on the little girl. He asked Megan if she wanted to come in to see his new puppy.

By 7:40 that evening, Megan had still not returned home. Her parents were increasingly concerned and a search of the neighborhood was begun. By 8:45, darkness was setting in and Megan was still unaccounted for. The police were called.

Going door to door on Barbara Lee Drive, the police spoke with neighbors on the street, including Jesse Timmendequas. Timmendequas denied any knowledge of what had happened to Megan, but he seemed nervous and refused to make eye contact with the investigating officer. Search dogs were soon brought in, but they failed to find a trail leading to the Timmendequas house. Efforts to find Megan went on continuously throughout the night without success.

The next day, police discovered incriminating evidence buried in trash left outside the house of Timmendequas. There was a portion of a waistband to a pair of children's shorts and other scraps of clothing. After the items were identified by Megan's mother, the police confronted Timmendequas. After hours of questioning, he eventually admitted to murdering Megan and dumping her body in the weeds at a local park.

Public outrage over the horrific crime was soon heightened when a local newspaper reported that Jesse Timmendequas had been twice convicted and imprisoned in the past for assaulting children.

When Timmendequas moved to Barbara Lee Drive in Hamilton, neither Megan's parents nor any of the other families on the block knew of his past — or the danger that he represented. The only people who did know about his secret past were the two other men he shared his house with — both were also alleged to be convicted sex offenders.

At first, Timmendequas denied to the police that he sexually attacked Megan. Then he admitted that he sexually attacked her, but minimized the extent of his assault on her. But when her autopsy results were returned, Timmendequas had no choice but to admit that in fact he had raped the little girl.

At this point, Megan's mother, Maureen, and father, Richard, only knew that they had suffered an unthinkable, heart-crushing loss — and that something was very, very wrong with a system that would let loose a Jesse Timmendequas on their daughter without warning. Something had to be done. If Megan's life was to have meaning, and other children like her were to be protected, the system would have to be fixed.

15

Megan's Law

The idea was simple, practical and overdue. So simple, so practical and so overdue that even the politicians got it. Here's the basic idea behind Megan's Law: *When a high-risk offender is released into a community, the community should be warned of the offender's presence.* Thanks to the unrelenting efforts of Megan's parents, Megan's Law was soon enacted in the state of New Jersey. The idea then caught political fire, gaining national media attention and further political momentum. The Kankas soon found themselves at the White House, watching President Clinton sign a national version into law on May 17, 1996. It was a deeply rewarding day for the Kankas — Megan would now never be forgotten and perhaps other children like her would be protected in the future. All in all, it was a very, very good day.

Megan's Law:
A Reality Check

Under the national version of Megan's Law, all fifty states now have a sex offender registry and community notification plan in effect. Now for a reality check: Not all states are created equal when it comes to putting Megan's Law to use. Some states have very strong

16

programs to notify the community and others very weak. The weak programs offer little or no protection to the public and are typically the result of constitutional concerns or legal challenges to Megan's Law. These are states where you'll want to rely upon the chapter "How to Identify Unregistered Sex Offenders". In essence, I'll show you alternative ways of accessing this information, outside of Megan's Law, that I have learned through my work as a private investigator.

On the exemplary side are states like California, where any citizen can go to local police stations and

President Clinton signs the federal version of Megan's Law into law on May 17, 1996. Onlookers include the Kanka family (far left). (Photo courtesy the White House.) Inset: Megan's last school photo, taken some nine months before her abduction. (Photo courtesy Maureen Kanka.)

browse a CD-ROM that contains profiles of 72,000 of the state's registered sex offenders. The computer program can be searched by name or by zip code if a community search is desired. California also has a 900 pay-per-call telephone information system that the public can also use to check the registry at the cost of ten dollars per call.

Other states with strong notification programs include Florida, where there's not only a hotline, but also an excellent Internet site with offender photographs and other information.

Other states, like Tennessee, have been hobbled by offender lawsuits that have challenged the constitutionality of the law.

To learn the specifics of how this information can be accessed in your state, refer to the chapter, "State by State Guide to Megan's Law", which is the heart of this book. If you live in a state with a weak community notification program, don't despair — you can still learn about the criminal history of any specific individual by using the chapter of this book, "How to Identify Unregistered Sex Offenders".

Name vs. Community Searches

There are two basic types of searches you may wish to conduct using Megan's Law — *name searches* and *community searches*. Depending on the implementation of Megan's Law in your own state, you may or may not be able to conduct either of these searches.

Name Searches

Use a *name search* when you have a specific person's name and want to learn if he (or she) is registered as a sex offender. Here are examples of scenarios under which you may wish to conduct a name search:

• You are hiring a new baby-sitter and Mary Smith has applied for the job. *Is Mary Smith a convicted child molester or some other type of registered sex offender?*

• You live in an apartment building. A new tenant is a lone male named John Smith. None of the other neighbors in the building knew John before he moved in and his background is a mystery. John seems to spend a lot of time hanging around the children in the building, befriending them and even buying them small gifts and treats. *Is John Smith a convicted child molester or other type of registered sex offender?*

19

• You're a single woman who met a promising man named John Smith in an online chat room on the Internet. You have a lot in common, have chatted and traded e-mails many times, and now he wants to take you out on a date. *Is John Smith a registered sex offender?*

Community Searches

Use a *community search* to learn if there are any registered sex offenders living in your immediate neighborhood, town, county or zip code.

Here are three scenarios under which you might want to opt for a community search:

• To raise money for an after-school program, your child and his classmates will be going door to door selling candy or other items. *Is there a registered sex offender living in the area whose door you don't want your child knocking on to sell candy?*

• You're a single woman who enjoys jogging both before and after work. *Are there any registered sex offenders living in your neighborhood whose faces and addresses you should become familiar with?*

• You were the victim of a sexual assault in the past. As

TUNNY, PATRICK J	
TURENTINE, JERRY L	
TURMAN, VERNON C	
TURNER, GARY R	
TURNER, JESSE G	
TURNER, MILTON W	122557
TURNER, STEVEN C	122964
TURPEN, ALLIE J	062852
TURPIN, RAYMOND E	091755
TURPIN, WENDELL T	051970
TUTTLE, MICHAEL D	101266
TWEDDELL, EDWARD L	030354
TYNER, MELVIN E	051139
TYSON, MICHAEL G	063066
ULREY, JERRY D	051252
UMPHREY, RONALD T	030173
UNDERHILL, NIEL	090559
UNDERWOOD, DALAN	110664
UNDERWOOD, LEON	061457
UPDEGRAFF, LOWELL	091139

Above is an excerpt from Indiana's sex offender registry identifying former world heavyweight champion boxer Mike Tyson as a registrant. Tyson was convicted of rape in 1992. The column of numbers on the right are dates of birth.

a result, you have a fear of being attacked again. As a proactive measure of self-defense, you want to learn: *Are there any registered sex offenders living nearby?*

The state that you live in will have everything to do with whether or not you can conduct a community search. The availability of a community search in your own state will be indicated in the chapter, "State by State Guide to Megan's Law".

If you want to run a name search or a community search or both, you will need to know about one more thing: *Personal Identifiers.* As you'll learn in the next chapter, these are the vital keys to making sure that you've got the right person and have not mistakenly identified an innocent person as a sex offender.

REGISTERED SEX OFFENDERS:
NAME SEARCHES

Here is a review of the steps needed to conduct a name search to determine if a person is a registered sex offender:

STEP ONE:

Look up your state in the chapter, "State by State Guide to Megan's Law" and determine if your state has enacted an effective version of Megan's Law. If your state has not, proceed to the chapter, "How to Identify Unregistered Sex Offenders."

STEP TWO:

If your state has an effective Megan's Law, check to see if the name of the person you are investigating is listed. If the name is not on the list, they are not a registered offender. However, you'll want to take note of the limitations of the sex offender registry in your state and also consider conducting a check to see if the person is an unregistered sex offender. If the name of the person you are checking *is* in the registry, proceed to step three.

STEP THREE:

Compare the personal identifiers provided by your state's sex offender registry with the personal identifiers of the person you are investigating. If two or more personal identifiers are matched, a positive identification has been made. If less than two personal identifiers are matched, a positive identification has not been made. If you do not have personal identifiers for the person you are investigating, see chapter, "Obtaining Personal Identifiers".

REGISTERED SEX OFFENDERS:
COMMUNITY SEARCHES

Here's a review of the steps needed to conduct a community search for registered sex offenders:

STEP ONE:

Look up your state in the chapter, "State by State Guide to Megan's Law" and determine whether your state has a sex offender registry which allows community searches. If it does not, there is no other way to reliably obtain this information.

STEP TWO:

If your state does allow community searches, follow the instructions in our "State by State Guide to Megan's Law" to receive information on registrants in a particular geographic area — usually city, county or zip code. However, also be sure to note the limitations of the sex offender registry in your state so that over reliance is not made on limited information.

WARNING!

If no registrants are identified in the community search, this does not necessarily mean that no registered sex offenders live in the area. Offenders who have failed to comply with change of address requirements or who recently moved into the area may not be identified.

Personal Identifiers: Getting the Right Person

Personal Identifiers: Getting the Right Person

With more than 273 million people now living in the United States, it goes without saying that many of us share the same name. This presents a key challenge in properly identifying previously convicted sex offenders.

Take this example: You are doing a background check on an individual named John Smith and you check your state's sex offender registry and learn that there's a registered sex offender by the name of John Smith. *How do you know if they are the same person, or two different people who just happen to have the same name?*

The answer is in using *personal identifiers*. A personal identifier is a piece of unique information that serves to more fully identify a person beyond his or her name. One example of a personal identifier is a person's date of birth. While there may be many John Smiths, there are far fewer with the same date of birth. **Ultimately, two or more personal identifiers MUST be matched before a positive identification can be made of a registered sex offender.**

Among the states that allow their sex offender registries to be checked by the general public, almost all provide one or more personal identifiers along with the registered sex offender's name. The purpose of the state providing personal identifiers is to further identify the registrants.

WARNING!

By not using personal identifiers to properly identify convicted sex offenders, the user of this book risks mistakenly identifying an innocent party as a sex offender! Two or more personal identifiers must be matched to make a conclusive identification!

Most Common
Personal Identifiers

Here are the most commonly used personal identifiers that you'll come across:

Full Legal Name
Photograph/Mug Shot
Date of Birth
Last Known Address
Social Security Number

Let's briefly return to our "John Smith" example from above. Say you are doing a background check on a person named John Smith. You've checked the sex offender registry in your state and sure enough, you've learned that there's a registrant named John Smith. The sex offender registry has provided two personal identifiers on John Smith. His *full legal name* is John Lowlife Smith and his *date of birth* is March 1, 1937. By comparing the personal identifiers of the registered sex offender John Smith with those of the John Smith you are checking on, you will be able to easily determine if they are one and the same, or two different people who happen to have the same name.

If you don't know the personal identifiers of the person you are investigating, you'll have to obtain them. The following chapter , "How to Obtain Personal Identifiers," explains where and how to obtain them.

Now let's take a brief look at the different types of personal identifiers and discuss the strengths and pitfalls of each.

Full Legal Name

Full legal names are very helpful. The most important component of a full legal name is the middle name. Middle initials are also helpful, but are not as conclusive as the actual full middle name. Suffixes, such as "Jr.", "Sr." and "III" are also important.

Unique spellings can also be very helpful. As an example, the name commonly spelled "Sean" might be uniquely spelled by a particular offender as "Shawon", "Shon" or "Shawn". These unique spellings, although not conclusive of identity, can be very helpful in moving toward a positive identification — or in eliminating innocent parties from consideration.

When obtaining information from your state's sex offender registry, be sure to keep an eye out for any aliases or nicknames associated with the known offender as well.

Photograph or Mug Shot

Photographs are an excellent and reliable method for making a positive identification. Fortunately, several states make photos or mugshots of registered sex offenders available. As mentioned earlier, in California they can be seen on a computer at many local police stations. Florida, Alaska and other states make photos available on the Internet. In many other states, flyers of locally registered sex offenders can be viewed by visiting a local police station.

Date of Birth

Dates of birth are one of the most reliable and commonly used personal identifiers. They are typically the first personal identifier, after full legal name, that is used by the criminal justice system.

Keep in mind that there is a critical distinction between a person's date of birth and what is commonly known as his birthday. A date of birth includes month, day *and* year of birth. A birthday is just month and day. We want to be relying upon only dates of birth, not birthdays.

Although it happens fairly infrequently, as a private investigator conducting background checks, I've run into situations where two people had the same name and   same birthday — but different dates of birth. Usually when this happens, you're dealing with a person who has a very common name like John Smith, Jose Sanchez or Robert Jones.

31

Last Known Address

Some states will provide the actual home address of a registered sex offender. Others won't, fearing that the offender might be targeted for harassment. In this case, often a general geographic location of the offender — such as zip code or city of residence — will be provided.

In states where the actual home address is provided, you have an excellent identifier. After all, there may be a thousand John Smiths in your state, but in all likelihood, there's only one John Smith (unless there's both a Jr. and Sr.) living at 123 Elm Street. The possibility of there being both a Jr. and Sr. at the same address is a good example of why we never rely upon just one personal identifier for positively identifying an offender.

Addresses do have one important shortcoming that you should be aware of. The offender is required to register every time he changes residence. Failure to re-register at a new address is usually a crime in and of itself which may land the offender back in prison. However, surprisingly, there's ample evidence that offenders often fail to keep their addresses up to date, despite the legal consequences of failing to do so. If the offender doesn't update his address, then the address obviously becomes of less value as an identifier.

On balance, a prudent approach would be to rely upon addresses for making a positive identification — but don't rely upon them for eliminating a person. For example, if the registry shows John Smith should be at 500 First Street, when he is in fact at 123 Elm Street, you shouldn't automatically assume that they are two different people. It's simply possible that Mr. Smith failed to notify authorities of his new address.

In states where the actual home address is not provided, but rather just a general geographic area, such as zip code, matching general geographic areas is not a reliable method of identification and should not be used. There could easily be many John Smiths in the same zip code. Relying upon a general area, such as zip code, could lead to the mistaken identification of an innocent party as a sex offender.

Social Security Number

Some states also use Social Security Numbers to identify registered sex offenders. Social Security Numbers make an excellent identifier due to their unique nature. In theory, there's just one Social Security Number per person. Social Security Numbers are always nine digits in the following sequence: xxx-xx-xxxx. The first three digits are a code that indicates the state where the number was first issued, as well as the year. (See the chart in the "Resource Kit" at the end of this book.)

The Social Security Administration, which issues the numbers, considers them to be private. Don't waste your time calling them to ask what somebody's Social Security Number is. In reality, Social Security Numbers aren't too private at all. There are many sources of public records, such as bankruptcy filings, where Social Security Numbers can be obtained. You'll learn how to obtain them in the following chapter, "Obtaining Personal Identifiers".

Other Personal Identifiers

There are other personal identifiers that are largely outside the scope of this book or are self-explanatory. They include:

Fingerprints
Physical Description
Tattoos
FBI Number
Place of Birth
Prior Addresses
Mother's Maiden Name

Obtaining Personal

Identifiers

Obtaining Personal Identifiers

By obtaining personal identifiers on the person you are investigating, you'll be able to compare them to those of a registered sex offender with the same name to determine whether they are the same person. To do this, you'll need to put on your detective's cap as some snooping — the legal kind — will be in order.

Let's look at two different scenarios — one in which you won't need this chapter and one in which you will.

In the first situation, let's say that you're doing a background check on good old John Smith. You check your state's sex offender registry and there are no John Smiths. You can therefore presume that Mr. Smith is not a registered sex offender. You can skip this section! Yes, it's that easy! (I should probably point out here that no technique is fool proof. This assumes that the true name of the person being investigated is "John Smith". If an offender is living under a false or changed name — probably an illegal act — then he would *not* be detected by these means.)

Now let's take a second example. In this case, you're doing a background check on a new assistant coach for your child's soccer team. The name of the assistant coach is John Smith and sure enough, a check of your state's sex offender registry shows a registered sex offender named John Smith living in your zip code. His home address is not public record. However, personal identifiers are available on registered sex offender John Smith. You've obtained his full legal name and date of birth. You're going to now try to obtain identifiers on assistant coach John Smith to see if they match those of the known registered sex offender.

This chapter teaches you the most likely places to obtain personal identifiers. Our example presumes that for whatever reason, you don't wish to simply come right out and ask the new assistant coach for his personal identifiers. Therefore, you'll be making some phone calls and checking public records to obtain his personal identifiers. *If at any point you feel that this is beyond your abilities – or, if you simply don't have time to do this detective work – you'll want to hire a private investigator for assistance.* This chapter ends with a brief explanation of how to go about hiring a P.I. and what his or her services should cost.

Application Forms

If you are lucky enough to have access to an employment, rental or membership application form for the
person you are investigating, you'll already have a
wealth of personal identifiers at your fingertips. Some
of the information that you'll find here will include:

Full Legal Name
Last Known Address
Prior Addresses
Date of Birth
Social Security Number

Voter Registration Records

Voter registration records are a valuable source for
obtaining a person's date of birth as well as full legal
name and prior addresses. Voter records are public
record in many states, but are off limits in others, due to
privacy concerns.

If voter registration records are public record in your
state, you might be able to obtain the date of birth of the
person you are investigating with just a phone call to the
local Board of Voter Registration. However, some voter
record offices may not provide information by phone

due to staff shortages. In these cases, you'll be required to make a trip to the local voter registration office to manually look up the records. Some of this information is also available over the Internet.

Start by calling 411 and asking the operator for the phone number of your local voter registration office. Call the number and use the following script as a guide to get the desired information. You'll be playing the part of the "Caller":

The Phone Call

INT. OFFICE - DAY

The telephone rings as the CALLER waits impatiently. Just then...

           Voter Clerk
Hello, voter registration.
May I help you?

           Caller
Hello. I'm wondering if
you could tell me if you
have a John Smith regis-
tered as a voter?

Voter Clerk
I'm sorry…but we don't
normally provide this
information by phone. However, we're not so busy
right now. Let me go to my
computer.

As the CALLER anxiously waits, the
soft tapping of fingers on keyboard
is heard through the receiver. Then…

Voter Clerk
Well, I can see we have
close to twenty John
Smiths here in Sample
County. Do you have an
address for him?

Caller
Why, yes, I do. He's liv-
ing on Shady Street in
Sampletown now…

Voter Clerk
Ahh, yes, here it is. 555
Shady Street. Yes, we have
him. He's registered.

> Caller
>
> Great. I just want to double check that we have the right person. Is there a middle name or initial?

> Voter Clerk
>
> Yes, his middle name is Lowlife.

> Caller
>
> Great, and his date of birth?

> Voter Clerk
>
> Mr. Smith was born March 1, 1937.

> Caller
>
> Great. That's all I need. Thank you very, very much!

The CALLER hangs up as a smile comes over his face: He's not only obtained the suspected offender's date of birth, but also another valuable identifier: A middle name!

Yes, it can be just this easy to obtain a person's date of birth and middle name. Of course, this assumes that the person has registered to vote at some time in the past.

If you're Internet savvy, you should also know about a website that sells voter registration records online. The site is located at *www.governmentrecords.com*. The current cost to search in a single state is $11 per name, whether or not a "hit" is received. One of the advantages to this is that you don't have to limit yourself to searching in a single county, but can instead search the entire state's records. Sites tend to come and go on the Internet — so let's hope this one is still up when you need it.

Phone Directories

Phone books are of limited value in obtaining identifiers — although they shouldn't be discounted altogether. Along with address information, a subject's middle name or middle initial can sometimes be obtained through this source. Local libraries may have old copies of phone books, which may be useful in ascertaining prior addresses.

DMV Records

In many states, Department of Motor Vehicles information is public record as well. In your state this agency may not be called the Department of Motor Vehicles. It may be called the Bureau of Motor Vehicles or something similar. Regardless, I'm talking about the government agency that hands out driver's licenses and license plates. As with voter registration records, DMV records may or may not be public record in your state due to privacy concerns.

If DMV information is available in your state, the information you can expect to obtain is:

Full Legal Name
Last Known Address
Date of Birth
Driver's License Number

There are a couple of pitfalls in obtaining DMV records that should make them a last resort on your checklist. The first pitfall is an inherent Catch 22. Your Department of Motor Vehicles won't typically release driver's license information on John Smith. Why? Because they have a thousand John Smiths. So, you'll be required to provide a name *plus* a date of birth and/or a driver's license number. Well, obviously, if you already have an identifier, then you wouldn't need to be contacting the DMV to start with!

STATES WHERE MOTOR VEHICLE RECORDS ARE RESTRICTED:

Records are not available to the public in these states:

California
Georgia
Virginia

Records are available in these states only with the signed consent of the person whose record you are obtaining:

Alaska
Arkansas
Connecticut
District of Columbia
Hawaii
Louisiana
Michigan
New Hampshire
New Jersey
North Dakota
Pennsylvania
Rhode Island
Washington
Wyoming

In certain situations, however, you might want to contact them. For example, if you have the driver's license number of the subject of the investigation, but not his actual date of birth. (Possibly you found a traffic ticket issued to him, which you'll learn how to do shortly. However, the traffic ticket only showed his driver's license number, not his date of birth.) By using the driver's license number you do have, you'll be able to obtain the subject's driver's license information, which will include his date of birth, as well as last known address and full legal name.

The second pitfall is that dealing directly with the DMV as a single, powerless citizen may be a very unpleasant experience.

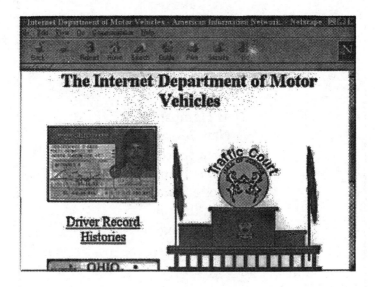

A do-it-yourself alternative would be to try the Internet DMV. This is a private business that brokers information from those states that allow public access to their DMV records. The cost is around $20 per search and will save you a million bucks worth of frustration. Their website is located at *www.ameri.com/dmv/dmv.htm*

Traffic Court Records

Traffic court records can be another rich source of personal identifiers. You'll have to play the phone game again with a government clerk. An in-person trip to the traffic court may also be necessary to dig through some court files. Information obtainable here includes:

Full Legal Name
Date of Birth
Driver's License Number
Last Known Address
Vehicle License Plate Number

Most cities have a traffic court for fast-track handling of parking tickets and non-felony driving violations. In almost every corner of the country, traffic court records are public record. This means that if you so choose, you can go down to the courthouse and lawfully request to see another person's traffic ticket.

Each traffic court has an *index*. An index is nothing more than a long, alphabetized list of persons who have had a case at the court; along with the date when the case was filed and the corresponding case number.

As you can imagine, these "indexes" are massive in scope as they include every person who's gotten a traffic ticket for as far back as the index goes. In most jurisdictions, this will be five, seven or ten years.

A typical court index is so massive that it's usually kept track of by computer, microfilm or microfiche (a form of microfilm).

You'll start by calling the traffic court to find out if the subject of your investigation has any cases on file there. If he does, you're going to visit the courthouse and review the court file to obtain whatever personal identifiers can be found.

However, be forewarned that some courts won't provide information by phone. They're too under-staffed to provide phone service and will make you go down to the court in person to check a name. As a P.I., my experience has been that the courts in big cities are the worst at providing phone information, and that the further out into small-town America you go, the better your chances will be of obtaining information.

Now, as you can imagine, this task is going to be more complicated when doing a background check on a subject named John Smith. When you call the court-house, you'll be told that there are a million cases under the name John Smith. The next most likely questions that the clerk will ask you are: "What is his date of birth?" or "What is his middle name?"

Obviously, if you don't have these, you're stuck in another Catch-22. As a fallback, if you have the address of the subject of your investigation, you might suggest it to the clerk as an identifier he or she could use.

You'll fare much better when conducting a name check on a subject with a unique name. Then there will likely be far fewer cases on file and the likelihood that one of them is the person you are investigating will be far greater.

Start by calling 411 and asking the operator for the telephone number for traffic court. If the operator says that there's no listing for traffic court, this may mean that in this area traffic cases are handled in the same court as low-level "misdemeanor" criminal matters.

Ask the operator for the number for the "Municipal Criminal Court" or just the criminal court. Depending on what area of the country you live in, this court may have another name. For example, in Nevada they're known as Justice Courts.

Once you've got the right phone number, call the court. In this example, let's make things a little easier by choosing a subject who has a less common name than our old friend "John Smith". Let's use the fictitious name "Oliver P. Deadwood III". The script for your phone call should go something like this:

The Phone Call 2

INT. OFFICE - DAY

The CALLER dials the phone number to traffic court and waits as the line is heard ringing on the other end. Just then:

>   Traffic Clerk
> Good afternoon. This is the
> Anytown Traffic Court. How
> can I help you?

>   Caller
> Good afternoon. Can you

check a name to see if any
traffic cases come up
under it?

                    Traffic Clerk
Yes. What is the name and
date of birth?

                    Caller
Well, actually, I don't
have a date of birth. However, it's an unusual
name. I highly doubt that
there's more than one person with this name.

                    Traffic Clerk
          (annoyed)
What is the name?

                    Caller
          (grateful)
Thank you...The name is
Oliver P. Deadwood III.

                    Traffic Clerk
One minute while I check.

Through the telephone receiver, the
CALLER can hear the sounds of fin-

gers typing at a keyboard. Then…

> Traffic Clerk
> I can see we have two
> cases for Oliver P. Dead-
> wood III. I can't tell
> you anything else over
> the phone. I can give you
> the case numbers. You're
> free to come down to the
> courthouse to view the
> files.

> Caller
> Sure, great!

The CALLER scribbles down the case
numbers as they are read off by the
TRAFFIC CLERK.

Now, wanna try a slick move? Since what you're
really after is a date of birth, you might be able to get
this information without actually going down to the
courthouse. Instead of thanking the clerk for his or her
time, continue the call like this:

The Phone Call 2, Continued:

> Caller
> This is great. I really

appreciate your help. By
the way, does a "D-O-B"
come up with those cases?

        Traffic Clerk
Yes, it does.

        Caller
Can I get that D-O-B?
I'll check it against
some information later
just to triple-check
that it's the right
person.

        Traffic Clerk
Sure. Mr. Deadwood's date
of birth is August 14,
1947.

        Caller
Great! Thank you for your
help. It's really appreci-
ated!

The CALLER hangs up his phone, a smug
look of satisfaction dawns across his
face.

Now, two brief notes. You'll notice we worked in

the term "D-O-B". (pronounced "Dee-Ohh-Bee"). This is legal system jargon for Date of Birth. By using it, the clerk you speak with will assume that you're part of the system as opposed to some yahoo on a fishing expedition. Either way, you have the same legal right to this information. However, in practice, court employees tend to give insiders better service than they give fresh-off-the-farm newbies.

On a second note, you'll notice that in our script the caller has always been friendly and courteous. Being nice will get you a long, long way when digging for dirt in the public records system. The clerks *never* go out of their way to help pushy, rude, demanding people. On the other hand, they just might go out of their way to help you if they think you're a nice person. So, even if you're not, fake it!

Now, let's assume for a moment that things didn't go quite as smoothly as they did in the above example. Let's assume that either the clerk refused to do a name check over the phone, or she did a name check and came up with some case numbers, but refused to provide the D.O.B. information. In either situation, you're headed to the courthouse. On page 67 is a mini-crash course to see you through your first trip to the courthouse, called *At the Courthouse: A Survival Guide*. In the meantime, let's keep looking at other options.

Divorce Records

Nationwide, approximately one out of every two marriages fail. This means that you've got a good chance of finding a divorce file for any adult subject. If the person has been divorced, there will be a court file that's available for public inspection. Inside may be found several personal identifiers, including:

Full Legal Name
Prior/Current Addresses
Social Security Numbers
Date of Birth

To get started, call directory assistance and ask for the phone number for the divorce court. In most parts of the country, there are upper and lower levels of the court system. Divorces are typically handled in the upper courts. Depending on what part of the country you live in, this upper court may be known as a superior, district or circuit court. In a few places, it is actually called Divorce Court. If the information operator comes up with several different court phone numbers, take the best sounding (non-criminal) one. Just call the number and ask whoever answers the phone if this is the right court for divorce records. If it's not, the clerk should be able to direct you to the right court.

Once you've gotten the right number, your phone call to the court should play out something like this:

```
INT. OFFICE - DAY

The Caller dials, and impatiently
waits as the line rings and rings and
rings. Finally...

          Court Clerk
     Hello, Clerk of Court.
     May I help you?

          Caller
     Hello. Is this the court
     that handles divorce
     cases?

          Court Clerk
     Among other things, yes,
     it is...

          Caller
     Great. Is it possible to
     do a name search to see
     if a person has any
     divorce cases?

          Court Clerk
     Yes, what's the name?
```

> Caller
John Lowlife Smith.

There's a lengthy pause as the Clerk searches her computer for cases...

> Court Clerk
Well, I can see that there is one divorce on file between John Lowlife Smith and Mary Smith.

> Caller
That's great. Can I get the case number and the date it was filed?

> Court Clerk
Of course. It was filed September 3, 1984. The case number is D14530.

> Caller
And where could I go to review the file?

> Court Clerk
Just come down to the court-house anytime between 8:30 a.m. and 4:30 p.m. and ask for the case number I gave

you. You'll be able to
review the file in our
viewing area.

                    Caller
     This is great. Thanks.
     I'm on my way now!

Click, the CALLER hangs up, looks at
his watch and grabs his car keys.

INT. COURTHOUSE - LATER THAT DAY

The CALLER is at the courthouse,
seated at a desk in the viewing room.
He's poring over a court file, jot-
ting down personal identifiers in a
notepad.

Now, just a brief final note about reviewing divorce
files: Not only can they be a source of personal identifiers, but they can also contain important additional
information about a person. For example, if the marriage failed because of physical or sexual abuse, these
allegations might be contained in the file. You might
want to take a few extra minutes to comb through the
material to look for this type of information.

Bankruptcy Court

Another court you'll want to know about is bankruptcy court, which is part of the federal court system. Scattered throughout America are nearly 200 bankruptcy courts where financially troubled people go to make a fresh start. When they do, they also typically leave behind a slew of personal information about themselves that is open to public scrutiny.

From our narrow point of view, bankruptcy court is a good place to find these personal identifiers:

Full Legal Name
Social Security Number
Last Known Address

Note that a person's date of birth will typically *not* be found in a bankruptcy filing.

There's an automated telephone information service in place for the nation's system of bankruptcy courts. In the following phone directory you'll notice many of the numbers are on the *VCIS* system. This stands for *Voice Case Information System*. Using a touch-tone phone, one can enter a person's name to learn if the person has had a bankruptcy filing at that specific court.

Directory of Bankruptcy Courts

Alabama, Northern District:
Decatur Division 205/353-2817
Birmingham Division 205/731-1614
Anniston Division 205/237-5631
Tuscaloosa Divison 205/752-0426
Alabama, Middle District 334/206-6300
Alabama, Southern District vcis 334/441-5637
Alaska vcis 907/271-2658
Arizona:
Phoenix Division vcis 602/640-5820
Tucson Division vcis 520/620-7475
Yuma Division 602/783-2288
Arkansas, Eastern District vcis 501/324-5770
vcis 800/891-6741
Arkansas, Western District vcis 501/324-5770
vcis 800/891-6741
California, Northern District:
San Jose Division vcis 800/457-0604
San Francisco Div. vcis 800/570-9819
vcis 415/705-3160
Oakland Division 510/273-7212
Santa Rosa Division 707/525-8539
California, Eastern vcis 800/736-0158
vcis 916/551-2989
California, Central District:
Los Angeles Division vcis 213/894-4111
San Fernando Division vcis 818/587-2936
Santa Ana Division vcis 714/836-2278
Santa Barbara Division vcis 805/899-7755
Riverside Division vcis 909/383-5552
California, Southern District
San Diego Division vcis 619/557-6521
Colorado vcis 303/844-0267
Connecticut vcis 203/240-3345
vcis 800/800-5113
Delaware vcis 888/667-5530
vcis 302/573-6233

Bankruptcy Courts

District of Columbia		202/273-0048
Florida, Northern District:		
Pensacola Division		904/435-8475
Tallahassee Division		904/942-8933
Florida, Middle District:		
Jacksonville Division	vcis	904/232-1313
Orlando Division	vcis	407/648-6800
Tampa Division	vcis	813/243-5210
Florida, Southern District	vcis	800/473-0226
	vcis	305/536-5979
Georgia, Northern District	vcis	404/730-2866
	vcis	404/730-2867
Georgia, Middle District	vcis	912/752-8183
Georgia, Southern District:		
Augusta Division		706/724-2421
Savannah Division		912/652-4100
Hawaii		808/541-1791
Idaho	vcis	208/334-9386
Illinois, Northern District:		
Chicago Division	vcis	312/408-5089
Rockford Division	vcis	815/987-4487
Illinois, Central District	vcis	217/492-4550
	vcis	800/827-9005
Illinois, Southern District	vcis	618/482-9365
	vcis	800/726-5622
Indiana, Northern District	vcis	800/726-5622
	vcis	219/236-8814
Indiana, Southern District	vcis	800/335-8003
Iowa, Northern District	vcis	800/249-9859
	vcis	319/362-9906
Iowa, Southern District	vcis	800/597-5917
	vcis	515/284-6230
Kansas	vcis	800/827-9028
	vcis	316/269-6668
Kentucky, Eastern	vcis	800/998-2650
	vcis	606/233-2657
Kentucky, Western	vcis	800/263-9385
	vcis	502/625-7391
Louisiana, Eastern	vcis	504/589-7879
Louisiana, Middle	vcis	504/382-2175
Louisiana, Western	vcis	800/326-4026
	vcis	318/676-4234
Maine	vcis	888/201-3572
	vcis	207/780-3755
Maryland	vcis	410/962-0733
Massachusetts	vcis	617/565-6025
Michigan, Eastern District		
(Includes Detroit)	vcis	313/961-4940
Michigan, Western District	vcis	616/456-2075

Bankruptcy Courts

Minnesota	vcis	800/959-9002
	vcis	612/290-4070
Mississippi, Northern District	vcis	601/369-8147
Mississippi, Southern District:		
Biloxi Division	vcis	800/293-2723
	vcis	601/435-2905
Jackson Division	vcis	800/601-8859
	vcis	601/965-6106
Missouri, Eastern District		
(includes St. Louis)	vcis	314/425-4054
Missouri, Western District	vcis	816/842-7985
Montana	vcis	406/782-1060
Nebraska	vcis	800/829-0112
	vcis	402/221-3757
Nevada:		
Las Vegas Division	vcis	800/314-3436
	vcis	702/388-6708
Reno Division		702/784-5515
New Hampshire	vcis	800/851-8954
	vcis	603/666-7424
New Jersey	vcis	201/645-6044
New Mexico	vcis	888/435-7822
	vcis	505/248-6536
New York, Northern District	vcis	800/206-1952
New York, Southern District:		
New York City Division	vcis	212/668-2772
White Plains Division		917/682-6117
New York, Eastern District	vcis	800/252-2537
	vcis	718/852-5726
New York, Western District	vcis	800/776-9578
	vcis	716/551-5311
North Carolina, Eastern District	vcis	919/234-7655
North Carolina, Middle District	vcis	910/333-5532
North Carolina, Western District	vcis	704/344-6311
North Dakota	vcis	701/239-5641
Ohio, Northern District	vcis	800/898-6899
	vcis	330/489-4731
	vcis	216/489-4771
Ohio, Southern District:		
Columbus Division	vcis	800/726-1006
	vcis	513/225-2562
Dayton Division	vcis	513/225-2544
Oklahoma, Northern District		918/581-7181
Oklahoma, Eastern District	vcis	918/756-8617
Oklahoma, Western District	vcis	800/872-1348
	vcis	405/231-4768
Oregon	vcis	800/726-2227
	vcis	503/326-2249
Pennsylvania, Eastern District	vcis	215/597-2244

Bankruptcy Courts

Pennsylvania, Middle District:
Harrisburg Division		717/782-2260
Wilkes-Barre Division		717/826-6450
Pennsylvania, Western District	vcis	412/355-3210
Rhode Island	vcis	401/528-4476
South Carolina	vcis	800/669-8767
	vcis	803/765-5211
South Dakota	vcis	800/768-6218
	vcis	605/330-4559
Tennessee, Eastern District	vcis	800/767-1512
	vcis	423/752-5272
Tennessee, Middle District		615/736-5584
Tennessee, Western District	vcis	888/381-4961
	vcis	901/544-4325

Texas, Northern District:
Amarillo Division		806/376-2302
Dallas Division	vcis	214/767-8092
Fort Worth Division		817/334-3802
Lubbock Division	vcis	214/767-8092
Texas, Southern District	vcis	800/745-4459
	vcis	713/250-5049
Texas, Eastern District	vcis	903/592-6119
Texas, Western District		
(includes San Antonio and		
El Paso)	vcis	210/229-4023
Utah	vcis	800/733-6740
	vcis	801/524-3107
Vermont	vcis	800/260-9956
	vcis	802/747-7627
Virginia, Eastern District	vcis	800/326-5879
Virginia, Western District:		
Harrisonburg Division		540/434-8327
Lynchburg Division		804/845-0317
Roanoke Division		540/857-2873
Washington, Eastern District		
(includes Spokane)		509/353-2404
Washington, Western District		
(includes Seattle)	vcis	888/436-7477
	vcis	206/553-8543
	vcis	206/442-6504
West Virginia, Northern District	vcis	304/233-7318
West Virginia, Southern District	vcis	304/347-5337
Wisconsin, Eastern District	vcis	414/297-3582
Wisconsin, Western District	vcis	800/743-8247
Wyoming		307/772-2037

As an important side note, you should know that the span of time covered by the system at each court varies and may not include older filings. Once a case is identified, you'll have to make a trip to the local bankruptcy court to review the actual file for the particulars. If the case is closed, you may have to request that the court retrieve the file from storage before making your trip to the courthouse.

In practical terms, you'll want to use bankruptcy court chiefly when you are in need of a Social Security Number for the subject of your investigation.

Marriage Licenses

Marriage licenses and/or marriage license applications are public record in most (but not all) places and might provide any or all of these identifiers:

Full Legal Name
Date of Birth
Place of Birth
Social Security Number
Mother's Maiden Name
Address

To research these, call your local information opera-

STATE OF CALIFORNIA
CERTIFICATION OF VITAL RECORD

COUNTY OF LOS ANGELES • REGISTRAR-RECORDER/ COUNTY CLERK

CERTIFICATE OF REGISTRY OF MARRIAGE
(PERSONAL DATA LICENSE TO MARRY CERTIFICATION OF MARRIAGE)

1934

GROOM PERSONAL DATA	ORENTHAL JAMES SIMPSON	DATE OF BIRTH 7-9-47
	AGE 37 NUMBER OF THIS MARRIAGE 2 DATE 4-16-80 DIVORCE	BIRTHPLACE CALIF.
	RESIDENCE OF GROOM 360 N. ROCKINGHAM	CITY OR TOWN WEST LOS ANGELES	COUNTY LOS ANGELES
	PRESENT OR LAST OCCUPATION SELF EMPLOYED	HIGHEST SCHOOL GRADE COMPLETED 15
	NAME OF FATHER OF GROOM JIMMY SIMPSON	MAIDEN NAME OF MOTHER OF GROOM EUNICE

BRIDE PERSONAL DATA	NICOLE BROWN	DATE OF BIRTH 5-19-59
	AGE 25 NUMBER OF THIS MARRIAGE 1	BIRTHPLACE GERMANY
	RESIDENCE OF BRIDE 360 N. ROCKINGHAM	CITY OR TOWN WEST LOS ANGELES	COUNTY LOS ANGELES
	PRESENT OR LAST OCCUPATION DECORATOR	HIGHEST SCHOOL GRADE COMPLETED 12	BIRTH NAME OF BRIDE SAME
	NAME OF FATHER OF BRIDE LOUIS H. BROWN	BIRTH NAME OF MOTHER OF BRIDE JUDITHA

AFFIDAVIT OF BRIDE AND GROOM

BRIDE SIGNATURE: Nicole Brown
GROOM SIGNATURE: O.J. Simpson

LICENSE TO MARRY

SUBSCRIBED AND SWORN TO BEFORE ME ON 1-30-85
DATE LICENSE ISSUED 1-30-85
EXPIRATION DATE 4-30-85
LICENSE NUMBER AE23706
COUNTY OF ISSUE OF LICENSE LOS ANGELES
COUNTY CLERK FRANK S. ZOLIN

WITNESSES
Tom Simpson 360 N Rockingham Ave Brentwood CA
Dominique Brown

CERTIFICATION OF PERSON PERFORMING CEREMONY
Feb. 2 85
Brentwood, Calif. LA
NAME OF PERSON PERFORMING CEREMONY Donn D. Moomaw PRESBYTERIAN MINISTER

DATE ACCEPTED FOR REGISTRATION FEB 03 85
LOCAL REGISTRAR-SIGNATURE 90049

This is to certify that this document is a true copy of the official record filed with the Registrar-Recorder/County Clerk.

Conny B. McCormack
CONNY B. McCORMACK
Registrar-Recorder/County Clerk

JAN 0 4 1999
19-665537

This copy not valid unless prepared on engraved border displaying the Seal and Signature of the Registrar-Recorder/County Clerk.

Above: The marriage license of O.J. Simpson and Nicole Brown. You'll note that this public record is rich in personal identifiers. (Identifiers of third parties have been redacted by author for privacy purposes.)

tor and ask for Marriage Licenses, which more often than not will be listed under such government offices as Vital Statistics or the County Recorder.

By calling the local marriage license office you'll be able to learn the availability of marriage license information. More than likely, a trip will be necessary to the local marriage license office where you'll have to ask the assistance of a government clerk in doing a name check to see if any licenses have been issued. As a brief side note, marriages licenses are usually issued by local government (city or county), as opposed to the state.

The previous page shows the 1985 marriage license of O.J. Simpson and Nicole Brown. As you can see, the document is rich in personal identifiers and other details. Identifiers available include O.J. Simpson's date of birth, place of birth, home address, and more.

There's one other marriage license source that you should know about, which is on the Internet. Clark County, Nevada is home to Las Vegas, marriage (and divorce) capital of America. At the county recorder's website, you can do a name search to see if a marriage license was issued. You can find the site at *www.co.clark.nv.us/recorder/mar_srch.htm.*

At the Courthouse: A Survival Guide

To the uninitiated, the courts can be bewildering and maybe even frightening. It's like being on a busy freeway where everybody seems to know where they're going – but you. Don't be intimidated! The courts are there for you as much as they are for the "regulars" of the legal system. The courts are a virtual gold mine of background information and personal identifiers that you won't want to do without.

The "regulars" represent many of the people you'll see at the courthouse. These are attorney service runners, law clerks, private investigators and attorneys who are in the process of filing, researching or copying official court records. The "regulars" can also be a source of help if you get lost. Don't be afraid to ask for help from anyone who looks like they know what they're doing — they can often save you a long wait in the wrong line.

Let's just take a quick overview of the courts. By knowing what to expect, you'll be better prepared mentally once you arrive there.

Different Types of Courts

There are several different types of courts — but they all function in essentially the same way. By mastering a few basic concepts, you'll be able to find your way around any courthouse.

In most cities, the various courts are located in either the same building or the same complex of buildings. You might consider the *criminal* courts as representing one half of the judicial system. The criminal half will itself be divided up into upper and lower systems. Felonies will be handled in the upper criminal courts and misdemeanors in the lower. Depending on what part of the country you are in, this upper court might be known as the Superior, District or Circuit court. The lower court might be known as the Municipal, District, or County court. Tagging along is traffic court — sometimes on its own and sometimes combined with the lower criminal court.

The other half of the judicial system is the *civil* court system. Generally, the civil court is where parties go to redress non-criminal matters such as money disputes and personal injury cases. In some areas, divorce cases are mixed in with the other civil cases; in other areas there are separate divorce courts.

68

As with the criminal side, the civil courts are usually divided into lower and upper courts. The lower courts are for smaller legal disputes, such as minor car accidents, and the upper courts are for major matters, such as wrongful death lawsuits. Below all of these are the small claims courts.

Now, regardless of the type of court you are obtaining information from — criminal, civil, traffic, divorce, or bankruptcy – the process will be basically the same.

At the Clerk of Court

When you arrive at the courthouse, you'll be making your way to the *Clerk of Court*. If you find yourself in a courtroom with lawyers, a judge and a court reporter, you're in the right building but wrong room. Your trip to the courthouse will not require you to enter an actual courtroom.

The Clerk of Court is the brain that runs the court system. It's the court administrative office that maintains the index system and stores old and new files. Remember, the *index system* is how the courts keep track of the thousands, or hundreds of thousands, of old and new court files. As stated before, it is really nothing more than an enormous alphabetized list of names under which court cases have been filed at some point in the past. The list will most likely either be computerized or on microfilm or microfiche. In the case of the latter, the court will have viewers set up nearby for your browsing pleasure.

Once you're at the Clerk of Court, you'll most likely have to get in line to speak with a court clerk who will be behind a counter. While you're waiting in line, take a quick scan around and see if any of the courthouse regulars I described earlier are in line nearby. If so, you might want to double-check that you're in the right line. Ask them, "Do you know if this is the right line to do a name check in?" If they're any type of courthouse pro, they'll be able to let you know if you're in the right line or not.

Once your wait in line is over and you find yourself face-to-face with a real live bonafide government clerk, *smile* (remember: niceness goes a *long* way!) and tell the clerk, "I need to do a name check."

Those are the only words you should need to say to clearly communicate your needs to the clerk. However, the clerk may sense that you're fresh off the farm and may ask a question in return, such as "What are you trying to do?"

In this case, your best answer is, "I'm trying to see if a person has any cases on file here." After hearing this, the only other question the clerk might have is, "What years do you need checked?" and your answer will be, "As many as possible!"

You may have noticed that the questions asked by the clerk in this encounter all revolved around identifying exactly what you needed. The questions never revolved around your right to see these records. *This is not and should never be an issue.* Court records, unless sealed by the court, are public record in the United States and can be viewed by any person who requests them.

The clerk will then let you know what the next step is. In some courts, the clerk will do the name look up for you. In other courts, computers are out where the public can access them. In still other courts, there are microfiche machines. These microfiche machines are fairly easy to use. You'll be required to load in a sheet of microfiche, which is nothing more than a square of plastic containing microscopic-sized printing. You'll then be able to see the names of persons with court cases. You'll scan forward to the name of the person you are investigating to see if there are any cases. If you need help, just ask a court employee or any courthouse regular how to operate it.

Regardless of how the index is checked at the particular court you go to, you'll need to walk away from this step of the process with three things:

Case Numbers (if any)
Filing Dates of Cases Found
Where to Go to Review Files

Usually, the same clerk who provides you with the name check or "index" information will also pull any actual court files found for you. The court files can vary in length from one or two pages up to thousands.

With court files in hand, the hard work has ended and the fun is about to begin! Inside the court file you'll be able to obtain all sorts of background information, including personal identifiers.

Once the clerk gives you the file(s), you'll make your way to a viewing area where there will be tables and chairs. Take a seat and go through the file carefully. In a relatively simple matter, like a traffic court case, you'll find the file to be small and easy to read. It will probably contain a copy of the original ticket. Look closely on it for personal identifiers. It should contain many or all of the following:

Full Legal Name
Date of Birth
Driver's License Number
Last Known Address
License Plate Number

If you've obtained any or all of the above, you're now an honorary detective! Congratulations! If the court file doesn't contain all of the personal identifiers you're in need of, consider visiting another court. If you started in traffic court and struck out, make your way to divorce court and try there. Once there, you'll just repeat the basic process:

1. Find the Clerk of the Court.
2. Do a name check.
3. Review any files found.

A few final words of advice: Don't be intimidated by the strange surroundings of the court system! But do go with a smile on your face. Be ready to clearly tell the clerks what you need and they'll tell you what to do from there.

Hiring a P.I.

Here's a scenario in which you might want to consider hiring a private investigator to help you out:

You've conducted a background check on a neighbor, an employee or other person to see if they're listed as a sex offender. Sure enough, there's a person with the same name listed as a registered sex offender. However, you've been unable to obtain enough identifiers on the person you are investigating to determine if he or she is the same person listed in the registry.

Obtaining personal identifiers on any given person is bread-and-butter work for an experienced private investigator. Depending on the area you live in, and the individual agency contacted, the cost of this limited investigation will likely be $100 to $200.

When you make contact with a local private investigator, be ready to tell him the purpose of your call and what information you have to work with.

As an example, if I were calling a P.I. for assistance, I might say:

"I'm conducting a background check on my new neighbor, John Smith. I've seen John approach and speak with my eight-year-old daughter several times. This makes me a little uncomfortable since I don't know anything about John and his background. I've checked the sex offender registry and sure enough, there's a John Smith listed. What I don't know is if they're the same person or two different people who happen to have the same name. Can you help me?"

A brief conversation will then likely ensue, with the P.I. asking you what identifiers you have on the John Smith in the sex offender registry and what identifiers, if any, you have on the John Smith who is your neighbor.

After learning what you have to go on, the P.I. should be able to give you an estimate for taking on the job. Once a price is agreed on, the P.I. may request a retainer in advance. If you're a new client, the retainer will likely be for the entire amount quoted.

F.Y.I.: Private investigators have access to many sources of information that the general public does not. For example, obtaining a person's Social Security Number requires little work for a P.I., as we are able to obtain these on our computers from information services we subscribe to. We also have access to other automated information, such as databases of persons' dates of birth, driver's license numbers and past and present addresses. However, you should know that to protect the privacy of third parties, the P.I. may not release the personal identifiers obtained directly to you. Rather, he may simply indicate whether or not they are a match to those of the known registered sex offender.

Finding a P.I.

Where does one find a P.I., anyway? Here are a few suggestions:

• If you have an attorney, ask him or her for a recommendation.

• Check the Yellow Pages, usually under "Investigators" or "Detectives". Make some calls around and see who you're comfortable with. If you speak to an investigator by phone and he or she is responsive to your questions, that probably means your business is wanted.

• On the Internet, go to your favorite search engine (such as my favorite, Hotbot, or Excite) and do a keyword search with the following terms: "private investigator" and "your town's name". If that doesn't produce satisfactory results, you might want to try one of several online directories of private investigators. Links to these directories can be found at *www.crimetime.com*.

You've now been tutored on how to obtain and use personal identifiers. It's time to put this knowledge to use. In the following chapter, you'll find the most comprehensive state-by-state guide to using Megan's Law ever published. Get started with it *now*!

Alabama through
Wyoming...

State by State Guide to Megan's Law

ALABAMA

INFORMATION AVAILABLE TO THE PUBLIC	Alabama makes the names of its sex offenders publicly available — but only if they were released after June 30, 1998. Someone released prior to this time might come up clean. See notes section.

COMMUNITY SEARCH AVAILABLE?	Yes

NAME SEARCH AVAILABLE?	Yes

LEGAL AUTHORITY	The Community Notification Act

EFFECTIVE DATE	May 1, 1998

| WHERE TO ACCESS INFO | On the Internet, visit the Alabama Department of Public Safety website at *www.gsiweb. net* where searches can be done by offender name, city or state.

Local police and sheriff stations maintain a publicly available file of prior community notification flyers which contain information on the offender's home address, numerous personal identifiers and the offense the person was previously convicted of.

Upon release of an offender, neighbors living within 1000, 1500 or 2000 feet (depending on area) of offender are to receive community notification flyers. |
|---|---|

ALABAMA

OFFENDERS WHO MUST REGISTER

Persons convicted of certain sex offenses who were released from incarceration, probation or parole after June 30, 1998.

Offenders must register for 25 years, repeat offenders for life.

OFFENDER PERSONAL IDENTIFIERS

Name
Home Address
Sex
Date of Birth
Physical Description
Photograph

AGENCY IN CHARGE

Alabama Bureau of Investigation
Attn.: Sex Offender Database
2720 Gunter Park Drive West #A
Montgomery, AL 36109

Telephone: 334-260-1100

NOTES

Because of the late June 30, 1998 start date, reliance on this information is strongly not recommended. See chapter "How to Identify Unregistered Sex Offenders".

The registry may also include juveniles, who are also subject to community notification based upon their risk to the community.

ALASKA

INFORMATION AVAILABLE TO THE PUBLIC

Alaska offers one of the very best sex offender registration and community notification programs in the nation. See detaials below.

COMMUNITY SEARCH AVAILABLE?	Yes
NAME SEARCH AVAILABLE?	Yes
LEGAL AUTHORITY	AS 18.65.087
EFFECTIVE DATE	January 1, 1996

WHERE TO ACCESS INFO

On the Internet, both name and community searches are available at Alaska's excellent website: *www.dps.state.ak.us/sorcr.*

Each Alaska State Trooper post also maintains a copy of the statewide registry, which is available for public inspection.

If you're not on the Internet, you can still call or write for information and the results will be mailed to you. Use the contact information in the Agency in Charge box on the opposite page. Both name and community searches are available.

ALASKA

OFFENDERS WHO MUST REGISTER

Persons convicted of certain sex offenses who were incarcerated, on probation, on parole or convicted on or after July 1, 1984.

First-time offenders must register for 15 years, second-time offenders for life.

OFFENDER PERSONAL IDENTIFIERS

Name
Address
Photograph
Place of Employment
Date of Birth

AGENCY IN CHARGE

Alaska State Troopers
Permits and Licensing Unit
5700 E. Tudor Road
Anchorage, AK 99507

Telephone: 907-269-0396

NOTES

Overall, Alaska offers one of the best programs in the country. There are now nearly 4,000 registrants in the state.

Information is also provided on an offender's crimes, date of crime and place of conviction.

ARIZONA

INFORMATION AVAILABLE TO THE PUBLIC

Information available to the public includes community notifications and a website, as of January 2000. *Over reliance on this information is not recommended, though.* See "Offenders Who Must Register" box for restrictions on the information.

COMMUNITY SEARCH AVAILABLE?	Yes
NAME SEARCH AVAILABLE?	Yes
LEGAL AUTHORITY	Ariz. Rev. Stat. §§ 13-3825
EFFECTIVE DATE	June 1, 1996

WHERE TO ACCESS INFO

Effective January 2000, a website makes both name and community searches available for moderate and high-risk offenders. Information available will include offender's photo and address. When available, access it through the Sexual Predator section at *www.crimetime.com.*

Local law enforcement agencies may also make notifications. For low-risk offenders, only other members of the household are notified. For medium and high-risk offenders, the neighborhood and other at-risk parties are notified through flyers and other means.

Phone and mail requests for offender information are not available.

84

ARIZONA

OFFENDERS WHO MUST REGISTER

Persons convicted of certain sex offenses who were released from incarceration or supervision on or after June 1, 1996 or were sentenced on or after this date. Three thousand offenders have registered since this date.

Offenders must register for life.

OFFENDER PERSONAL IDENTIFIERS

Full Legal Name
Photograph
Address
Physical Description

AGENCY IN CHARGE

Arizona Dept. of Public Safety
Attn.: Sex Offender Unit
P.O. Box 6638
Phoenix, AZ 85005-6638

Telephone: 602-255-0611

NOTES

The June 1, 1996 trigger date for registration leaves a lot of offenders free from being publicly identified. Advice: Use this program as a back-up, but follow techniques in the chapter "How to Identify Unregistered Sex Offenders".

ARKANSAS

INFORMATION AVAILABLE TO THE PUBLIC

Information available to the public in Arkansas is very limited and consists of arbitrary law enforcement notification of the public. Neither name nor community searches are available.

COMMUNITY SEARCH AVAILABLE?	No

NAME SEARCH AVAILABLE?	No

LEGAL AUTHORITY	Sex and Child Offender Registration Act of 1997

EFFECTIVE DATE	August 1, 1997

WHERE TO ACCESS INFO

This information is not available to the public in Arkansas, except when released at the discretion of local law enforcement agencies. Release of information typically includes flyers with offender information.

Mail, phone and Internet requests for offender information are not available.

ARKANSAS

OFFENDERS WHO MUST REGISTER

Persons who were convicted, incarcerated, on probation or on parole on August 1, 1997 or later. Stalking is also included as a registerable offense.

Offenders must register for 15 years, sexually violent predators for 20.

OFFENDER PERSONAL IDENTIFIERS

Full Legal Name*
Photograph*
Location*

* At discretion of local law enforcement agencies.

AGENCY IN CHARGE

Arkansas Crime Information Center
One Capital Mall
Little Rock, AR 72201

Telephone: 501-682-2222

NOTES

Reliance on this limited information is not recommended. See chapter "How to Identify Unregistered Sex offenders".

The state currently has approximately 2,000 registrants.

CALIFORNIA

INFORMATION AVAILABLE TO THE PUBLIC	
	California has the largest registry of sex offenders in the nation — 84,000 plus names. All but 12,419 are public record. The California sex offender registry is widely open to the public under Megan's Law.

COMMUNITY SEARCH AVAILABLE?	Yes

NAME SEARCH AVAILABLE?	Yes

LEGAL AUTHORITY	Cal. Penal Code §§ 290-291

EFFECTIVE DATE	September 26, 1996

WHERE TO ACCESS INFO

Many police and sheriff stations have a public access computer containing a CD-ROM with information on the state's "serious offenders" and "high-risk offenders" — the worst of the worst. (These two categories account for approximately 72,000 of the state's 84,000 plus registrants.) It's updated four times a year. Offender zip codes, but not street addresses, are included. Photos are posted for approximately 65% of the offenders. Both name and community searches are available. Users must show identification and sign a form before accessing the CD-ROM. *Free.*

The *Sex Offender Identification Line* is a "900" pay-per-call line now offering the same information. (Previously it was limited to child molesters only.) The cost is $10 per call; two names can be checked per call. Information is for "protecting persons at risk" only and is prohibited from being used for insurance, loan, credit, employment, education, housing or business purposes. Call 900-463-0400.

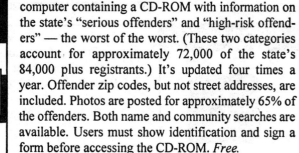

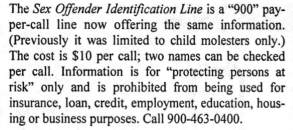

CALIFORNIA

OFFENDERS WHO MUST REGISTER

Persons convicted of certain sex offenses since 1947. The state has maintained its registry since this time, but it only became public record in 1996.

Offenders must register for life.

OFFENDER PERSONAL IDENTIFIERS

Full Legal Name
Known Aliases
Gender & Race
Physical Description
Photograph
Date of Birth
Zip Code, Not Address

AGENCY IN CHARGE

California Dept. of Justice
Attn.: Sex Offender Reg. Program
P.O. Box 944255
Sacramento, CA 94244-2550

Telephone: 900-463-0400
($10 per call)

NOTES

California's official sex offender registry is NOT available on the Internet. Be wary of unofficial sites with unofficial and incomplete information.

Registered sex offenders are required to provide blood samples for inclusion in the state's violent offender DNA database.

Law enforcement agencies may proactively notify the community with flyers and other means when a serious or high-risk offender is present.

COLORADO

INFORMATION AVAILABLE TO THE PUBLIC

Access to Colorado's sex offender registry by the public is very limited. Statewide name searches are not available. Local police agencies may release some information. See details below.

COMMUNITY SEARCH AVAILABLE?	Yes
NAME SEARCH AVAILABLE?	No
LEGAL AUTHORITY	Sex Offender Registry Statute
EFFECTIVE DATE	July 1, 1994

WHERE TO ACCESS INFO

Name searches of the statewide registry are not available. Phone, Internet or mail requests for offender information are not available.

Local law enforcement agencies are authorized to release information on offenders registered in their jurisdiction. A name can be checked or a list of locally registered offenders can be viewed. Police agencies have information on offenders in their municipality; sheriff departments have information on offenders living in unincorporated areas only.

90

COLORADO

OFFENDERS WHO MUST REGISTER

Persons convicted of certain sex offenses on or after July 1, 1994.

Depending on the severity of the original offense, registrants are required to be registered for 5, 10 or 20 years.

OFFENDER PERSONAL IDENTIFIERS

Full Legal Name
Physical Description
Address
Date of Birth

AGENCY IN CHARGE

Colorado Bureau of Investigation
Attn.: Sex Offender Registry
690 Kipling Street., Suite 3000
Lakewood, CO 80215

Telephone: 303-239-4222

NOTES

Reliance on Colorado's limited sex offender registration program is not recommended. See chapter "How to Identify Unregistered Sex Offenders" for instructions on obtaining a person's criminal record. Fortunately, Colorado is a state where this is possible. This is highly recommended.

Before hiring new employees, nursing care facilities must have the Colorado Bureau of Investigation check the registry.

CONNECTICUT

INFORMATION AVAILABLE TO THE PUBLIC

The state's registry is open to the public with access available through several different means. Includes 2,000 plus names. See details below.

COMMUNITY SEARCH AVAILABLE?	Yes

NAME SEARCH AVAILABLE?	Yes

LEGAL AUTHORITY	Public Act No. 98-111

EFFECTIVE DATE	October 1, 1998

WHERE TO ACCESS INFO

On the Internet, the registry can be searched by offender name, zip code or town name. Find it at the Sexual Predator section at *www.crimetime.com* or directly at *www.state.ct.us/dps*.

Each local police department and state trooper station maintains a file of locally registered offenders which is available for public viewing. Some state police troops also have public access computers where the statewide registry can be checked via the Internet.

Name searches can also be done by phone. Call 860-685-8060.

Law enforcement agencies may also notify the public about high-risk registrants.

CONNECTICUT

OFFENDERS WHO MUST REGISTER

Persons convicted of certain sex offenses who were released into the community on or after October 1, 1988.

Offenders must register for ten years, sexually violent offenders for life.

OFFENDER PERSONAL IDENTIFIERS

Name
Date of Birth
Address
Photograph
Physical Description

AGENCY IN CHARGE

Department of Public Safety
Sex Offender Registry Unit
1111 Country Club Road
Middletown, CT 06457-9294

Telephone: 860-685-8060

NOTES

When doing a name search, use the statewide registry, not a local law enforcement agency. Why? If the offender hasn't registered, he won't show up in the local file, but will in the statewide registry.

Violent offender addresses are verified every three months; other offenders once per year. Failure to register is a Class D felony.

DELAWARE

INFORMATION AVAILABLE TO THE PUBLIC

Delaware now makes its sex offender information available to the public, but this only includes persons convicted after June 24, 1994. *Sole reliance on this limited information is not recommended.* See chapter "How to Identify Unregistered Sex Offenders".

COMMUNITY SEARCH AVAILABLE?	Yes
NAME SEARCH AVAILABLE?	Yes
LEGAL AUTHORITY	Title 11, Sec. 4120 & 4121
EFFECTIVE DATE	June 24, 1994

WHERE TO ACCESS INFO

On the Internet, searches can be done by name, city, development or zip. Find it in the Sexual Predator section at *www.crimetime.com* or at *www.state.de.us/dsp/sexoff/*.

Local police may go door-to-door with flyers if a high risk offender is present.

Mail and telephone requests for offender information are not available.

DELAWARE

OFFENDERS WHO MUST REGISTER

Offenders convicted after June 24, 1994 of certain sex offenses.

Offenders must register for life.

OFFENDER PERSONAL IDENTIFIERS

Name
Photograph
Registration Address
Date of Birth
Physical Description

AGENCY IN CHARGE

State Bureau of Investigation
Sex Offender Central Registry
P.O. Box 430
Dover, DE 19903

Telephone: 302-739-5882

NOTES

When checking into the background of a particular individual in Delaware, you'll want to use the chapter "How to Identify Unregistered Sex Offenders".

DISTRICT OF COLUMBIA

INFORMATION AVAILABLE TO THE PUBLIC

As of our press date, the District of Columbia had still not put a working Megan's Law into effect.

COMMUNITY SEARCH AVAILABLE?	TBD
NAME SEARCH AVAILABLE?	TBD
LEGAL AUTHORITY	TBD
EFFECTIVE DATE	TBD

WHERE TO ACCESS INFO

There is presently no public access. On 8-4-99 emergency legislation was passed authorizing sex offender registration and community notification until such time as a permanent law could be passed. However, under the emergency law no registrations or notifications have taken place.

DISTRICT OF COLUMBIA

OFFENDERS WHO MUST REGISTER

To be determined.

OFFENDER PERSONAL IDENTIFIERS

To be determined.

AGENCY IN CHARGE

D.C. Metropolitan Police Dept.
Attn.: Sex Offender Registration
200 Indiana Ave., N.W.
Washington, D.C. 20001

Telephone: 202-727-4409

NOTES

See chapter "How to Identify Unregistered Sex Offenders" for instructions on doing a criminal check on someone on D.C. Unfortunately, though, this will not identify any convictions outside of the city.

FLORIDA

INFORMATION AVAILABLE TO THE PUBLIC

Florida offers one of the very best versions of Megan's Law in the country. The public can openly access the state's information several different ways. See details below.

COMMUNITY SEARCH AVAILABLE?	Yes
NAME SEARCH AVAILABLE?	Yes
LEGAL AUTHORITY	Florida Public Safety Information Act
EFFECTIVE DATE	October 1, 1997

WHERE TO ACCESS INFO

On the Internet, conduct name or community searches at the Florida Department of Law Enforcement's website. You can get there via the Sexual Predator section at *www.crimetime.com* or directly at *www.fdle.state.fl.us* and then follow the links to the Sexual Predator section.

To access offender information by phone, call 1-888-FL Predator (1-888-357-7332) from within the state. If you're outside of Florida, call 850-410-8572.

To receive a free list of offenders in one particular zip code, mail or telephone your request to the FDLE (see info next page).

98

FLORIDA

OFFENDERS WHO MUST REGISTER

Predators whose offense occurred on or after October 1, 1993 which resulted in a conviction. Offenders who were released from incarceration, probation or parole on or after October 1, 1997. Conducting a criminal history in the state to obtain older convictions is recommended.

Offenders must register for 20 years, sexual predators, indefinitely unless relieved by a court.

OFFENDER PERSONAL IDENTIFIERS

Full Legal Name
Aliases
Mug Shot
Date of Birth
Last Reported Address
Physical Description

AGENCY IN CHARGE

Florida Dept. of Law Enforcement
Sexual Offender/Predator Unit
P.O. Box 1489
Tallahassee, FL 32302-1489

Telephone: 1-888-FL Predator
(Outside Florida): 850-410-8572

NOTES

Predators are forbidden from working with minors — in either a professional or volunteer setting. When a sexual predator moves to a new area, local law enforcement is to notify area schools and daycare centers within a one mile radius.

99

GEORGIA

INFORMATION AVAILABLE TO THE PUBLIC

Georgia's sex offender registry is open to the public. However, it only includes persons released from prison, probation, or parole after July 1, 1996. *Sole reliance on this limited information is not recommended.* See chapter "How to Identify Unregistered Sex Offenders".

COMMUNITY SEARCH AVAILABLE?	Yes

NAME SEARCH AVAILABLE?	Yes

LEGAL AUTHORITY	O.C.G.A. 42-1-12

EFFECTIVE DATE	July 1, 1996

WHERE TO ACCESS INFO

On the Internet, the registry is searchable by offender's name, city, county or zip code. Access via the Sexual Predator section at *www.crimetime.com* or directly at: *www.ganet.org/gbi.*

Information on locally registered offenders is kept on file at local sheriff's departments for viewing by the public.

Phone or mail requests are not available.

GEORGIA

OFFENDERS WHO MUST REGISTER

Any convicted sex offender who was released from prison, probation or parole after July 1, 1996.

Sex offenders are required to register for 10 years. Sexual predators are required to register for life.

OFFENDER PERSONAL IDENTIFIERS

Full Legal Name
Registration Address
Date of Birth
Physical Description

AGENCY IN CHARGE

Georgia Bureau of Investigation
Attn.: GCIC
P.O. Box 370748
Decatur, GA 30037-0748

Telephone: 404-244-2601

NOTES

Because of the late 1996 start date, further investigation is recommended. See chapter "How to Identify Unregistered Sex Offenders" for information on identifying pre-1996 convictions.

Georgia currently has over 3,000 registered offenders.

HAWAII

Hawaii's sex offender registry is public record and includes both name and community searches. However, pre-1997 information may be incomplete.

COMMUNITY SEARCH AVAILABLE?	Yes
NAME SEARCH AVAILABLE?	Yes
LEGAL AUTHORITY	Act 316 SLH 1997
EFFECTIVE DATE	July 1, 1997

WHERE TO ACCESS INFO

Public-access computer terminals are available at the Hawaii Criminal Justice Data Center (address on opposite page) as well as at main county police stations. The computers can be used to look up names, and to do community searches by street and/or zip code. Also available for viewing is a book of mug shots.

For a $15 fee, mail-in requests are also accepted. Send the name of the person to be checked to the address on the opposite page.

Neither phone nor website look ups are available.

HAWAII

OFFENDERS WHO MUST REGISTER

Although the present law took effect in 1997, it includes sex offenders who were registered under the state's prior county-level program. However, pre-1997 data may be incomplete and should not be solely relied upon.

Sex offenders must register for life in Hawaii.

OFFENDER PERSONAL IDENTIFIERS

Name
Street Name and Zip Code
Photograph
Vehicle Description

AGENCY IN CHARGE

Hawaii Criminal Justice Data Center
465 S. King Street, Rm 101
Honolulu, HI 96813

Telephone: 808-587-3100

NOTES

Hawaii allows public access to statewide criminal conviction histories. See "How to Identify Unregistered Sex Offenders" for details on delving further into any given person's possible criminal history. This will circumvent the questionable pre-1997 data.

103

IDAHO

INFORMATION AVAILABLE TO THE PUBLIC

Idaho's sex offender registry is open to the public. Sole reliance on this limited information is not recommended due to the 1993 start date. See chapter "How to Identify Unregistered Sex Offenders".

COMMUNITY SEARCH AVAILABLE?	Yes
NAME SEARCH AVAILABLE?	Yes
LEGAL AUTHORITY	Sex Offender Registration Act
EFFECTIVE DATE	July 1, 1993

WHERE TO ACCESS INFO

At local sheriff's departments, access to the statewide database of offenders is available to the public. Name searches can be run, as well as community searches by county or zip code.

By mail, names will be checked when submitted to the Bureau of Criminal Identification (see address next page). There's no charge. Be sure to include the offender's name and as many identifiers as possible, including date of birth, Social Security Number and address. They prefer requests be made on their form, *Central Sex Offender Registry Request for Public Information*, which can be obtained at local sheriff's offices or by calling 208-884-7305. Offender photos can be obtained for an additional $5.

IDAHO

OFFENDERS WHO MUST REGISTER

The registry includes persons who were incarcerated or on probation or parole as of July 1, 1993, or were convicted after this date.

Registrants who have been arrest free for 10 years are eligible to apply for relief from registration.

OFFENDER PERSONAL IDENTIFIERS

Full Legal Name
Address
Aliases
Date of Birth

AGENCY IN CHARGE

Idaho State Police
Bureau of Criminal Identification
P.O. Box 700
Meridian, ID 83680-0700

Telephone: 208-884-7305

NOTES

Persons making offender information requests must provide their name, address, and driver's license number or SSN.

Look for a website to go up with this information in the year 2000.

Juvenile offenders between the ages of 14 and 17 are required to register.

ILLINOIS

INFORMATION AVAILABLE TO THE PUBLIC

The Illinois sex offender registry is available to the public via the Internet and at local police agencies. The state presently has 14,500 registrants.

COMMUNITY SEARCH AVAILABLE?	Yes
NAME SEARCH AVAILABLE?	Yes
LEGAL AUTHORITY	Sex Offender Registration Act
EFFECTIVE DATE	July 1, 1999

WHERE TO ACCESS INFO

Local police and sheriff's stations maintain a public list of offenders who are required to register in that county. Some individual cities, including Chicago, have put their lists on the Internet. Find these links in the Sexual Predator section at *www.crimetime.com*.

By late 1999, the Illinois State Patrol should have the entire state's database of offenders on the Internet. Find it via *www.crimetime.com* or try it directly at: *www.state.il.us/ isp/isphpage.htm*.

Mail or phone look ups of offender information are not available.

ILLINOIS

OFFENDERS WHO MUST REGISTER

Persons convicted of certain sex offenses who were released from prison, probation or parole within the past 10 years.

Offenders must register for 10 years, sexual predators for life.

OFFENDER PERSONAL IDENTIFIERS

Full Legal Name
Photograph
Date of Birth
Street of Residence
Physical Description

AGENCY IN CHARGE

Illinois State Police
Attn.: Sex Offender Reg. Unit
400 Iles Park Place, Suite 140
Springfield, IL 62718

Telephone: 217-785-0653

NOTES

Failure of an offender to properly register may result in an additional 10 years of registration.

The list is also distributed to local schools and child care facilities.

INDIANA

INFORMATION AVAILABLE TO THE PUBLIC

Indiana's sex offender registry is open to the public. Name searches are available several different ways. Community searches are not available.

COMMUNITY SEARCH AVAILABLE?	No
NAME SEARCH AVAILABLE?	Yes
LEGAL AUTHORITY	P.C. 11-1994, et al.
EFFECTIVE DATE	July 1, 1994

WHERE TO ACCESS INFO

On the Internet, name searches can be conducted. Get there via the Sexual Predator section at *www.crimetime.com* or directly at: *www.state.in.us/cji/html/sexoffender.html*.

Indiana will also do a name look up by phone. Call 317-232-1233.

Look ups can also be requested by mail. Send your request to the "Agency in Charge" on the opposite page.

INDIANA

OFFENDERS WHO MUST REGISTER

Includes offenders convicted of certain sex offenses who were released from incarceration, probation or parole since 1989. Prior to 1989, the registry includes State Police records going back 75 years.

Offenders convicted since June 30, 1994 must register locally — sex offenders for 10 years, sexual predators indefinitely.

OFFENDER PERSONAL IDENTIFIERS

Name
Aliases
Date of Birth
Physical Description
Social Security Number

AGENCY IN CHARGE

Indiana Criminal Justice Institute
302 West Washington Street
Room E-209
Indianapolis, IN 46204

Telephone: 317-232-1233

NOTES

The list of sex offenders is also mailed out to local schools, child care facilities, libraries and other organizations.

Be sure to use personal identifiers to correctly identify offenders!

IOWA

The Iowa sex offender registry is open to the public in limited form. Name checks can be done, but not community searches. See details below.

COMMUNITY SEARCH AVAILABLE?	No
NAME SEARCH AVAILABLE?	Yes
LEGAL AUTHORITY	Code of Iowa, Chapter 692A
EFFECTIVE DATE	July 1, 1995

WHERE TO ACCESS INFO

The Iowa sex offender registry can be searched at any one of the state's 99 sheriff's departments. You'll have to complete form DCI-150 (*Request for Registry Information*) and provide the name *and* address of the person you are investigating. Authorities will indicate a "hit" only if both the offender name and address on file match with the offender name and address you provide.

There is no Internet, mail or telephone look up available.

IOWA

OFFENDERS WHO MUST REGISTER

Persons convicted of certain sex offenses who were convicted, incarcerated, or on probation or parole on or after July 1, 1995.

Offenders are required to register for 10 years, sexual predators indefinitely. Failure to register is grounds for automatic revocation of probation or parole.

OFFENDER PERSONAL IDENTIFIERS

Name
Address
Physical Description

AGENCY IN CHARGE

Sex Offender Registry
Iowa Div. of Criminal Investigation
Wallace State Office Building
Des Moines, IA 50319

Telephone: 515-281-5138

NOTES

Due to the late July 1, 1995 start date, investigation to determine if the person is an unregistered sex offender is highly recommended. See chapter "How to Identify Unregistered Sex Offenders".

111

KANSAS

| INFORMATION AVAILABLE TO THE PUBLIC | The Kansas sex offender registry is open to the public. However, due to a Kansas Supreme Court decision, only offenders who committed their offenses after April 14, 1994 are included. Use of techniques described in chapter "How to Identify Unregistered Sex Offenders" is strongly urged. |

COMMUNITY SEARCH AVAILABLE?	Yes
NAME SEARCH AVAILABLE?	Yes
LEGAL AUTHORITY	K.S.A. 22-4901
EFFECTIVE DATE	April 14, 1994

WHERE TO ACCESS INFO

On the Internet, information is searchable by name, city, county or zip code. Access it via the Sexual Predator section at *www.crimetime.com* or directly at *www.ink.org/public/kbi.html.*

Name look ups can be obtained by phone. Call 785-296-6656 between 8 a.m. and 5 p.m.

Mail requests for offender information can be obtained by writing to the address on the facing page. There's no fee.

Every sheriff's station also maintains public information on offenders registered locally in that particular county.

KANSAS

OFFENDERS WHO MUST REGISTER

Offenders who committed certain sex offenses after April 14, 1994 must register.

Offenders must register for 10 years, but can apply to a court for release from registration prior to this. The court must hold a hearing to determine whether the offender is rehabilitated.

OFFENDER PERSONAL IDENTIFIERS

Full Legal Name
Last Known Address
County
Race/Sex
Date of Birth

AGENCY IN CHARGE

Kansas Bureau of Investigation
Crime Data Information Center
1620 S.W. Tyler
Topeka, KS 66612-1837

Telephone: 785-296-6656

NOTES

Sole reliance on this limited information is not recommended due to the 1994 start date. See chapter "How to Identify Unregistered Sex Offenders" to identify crimes which may have been committed earlier than this by the person you are investigating.

KENTUCKY

INFORMATION AVAILABLE TO THE PUBLIC

Kentucky was one of the last states to put its own version of Megan's Law into effect — and it turned out to be *not* worth the wait. The state offers one of the weakest Megan's Laws in the nation. *Reliance on this limited information is not recommended.* See chapter "How to Identify Unregistered Sex Offenders".

COMMUNITY SEARCH AVAILABLE?	No
NAME SEARCH AVAILABLE?	No
LEGAL AUTHORITY	K.R.S. 17.572
EFFECTIVE DATE	January 15, 1999

WHERE TO ACCESS INFO

Offender information is not available by phone, mail or Interent.

Sheriffs are authorized to release information on released high-risk offenders to the news media and "interested persons" in the community.

KENTUCKY

OFFENDERS WHO MUST REGISTER

Persons convicted of certain sex offenses who were released from incarceration on or after January 15, 1999.

Offenders must register for a minimum of 10 years.

OFFENDER PERSONAL IDENTIFIERS

Name
Aliases
Address
Photograph (if available)
Physical Description
Date of Birth
Vehicle Description

AGENCY IN CHARGE

Kentucky State Police
Attn.: Records Section
1250 Louisville Rd.
Frankfort, KY 40601

Telephone: 502-227-8700

NOTES

Fortunately, Kentucky is a state that allows access to another person's statewide criminal history. When investigating a particular individual, you'll want to go this route. See chapter "How to Identify Unregistered Sex Offenders".

LOUISIANA

INFORMATION AVAILABLE TO THE PUBLIC

Louisiana's sex offender registry is open to the public, but only contains information on persons convicted since July 1, 1997. *Sole reliance on this limited information is not recommended.* See chapter "How to Identify Unregistered Sex Offenders".

COMMUNITY SEARCH AVAILABLE?	No*
NAME SEARCH AVAILABLE?	Yes
LEGAL AUTHORITY	Louisiana Statute 15.542
EFFECTIVE DATE	July 1, 1997

WHERE TO ACCESS INFO

Name look ups can be obtained by calling 1-800-858-0551 between 8 a.m. and 4:30 p.m.

Name searches can also be done by mail. There's no charge. Send your request to the address in the "Agency in Charge" box on next page.

*A website is scheduled to go up in early 2000. Community searches will be available at the website. Link to it via the Sexual Predator section at *www.crimetime.com* when available.

OFFENDERS WHO MUST REGISTER

Persons convicted of certain sex offenses on or after July 1, 1997.

Offenders must register annually for 10 years. Sexually violent predators must register every 90 days for life.

OFFENDER PERSONAL IDENTIFIERS

Full Legal Name
Address
Date of Birth
Physical Description

AGENCY IN CHARGE

Louisiana State Police
Bureau of Criminal Identification and Information
P.O. Box 66614
Baton Rouge, LA 70896

Telephone: 1-800-858-0551

NOTES

Due to the late 1997 start date, you'll want to delve further into the criminal history, if any, of the person you are investigating. See chapter "How to Identify Unregistered Sex Offenders".

MAINE

INFORMATION AVAILABLE TO THE PUBLIC

The Maine sex offender registry is open to the public. There are two different groups of offenders required to register, each with a different entry date into the system. See the Offenders Who Must Register box on next page. There are less than 300 names on the entire list.

COMMUNITY SEARCH AVAILABLE?

Yes

NAME SEARCH AVAILABLE?

Yes

LEGAL AUTHORITY

Sex Offender Registration and Notification Act

EFFECTIVE DATE

June 30, 1992 and September 18, 1999

WHERE TO ACCESS INFO

Name searches are available by telephone. Call 207-624-7009.

Information is also available by mail. Single name look ups can be run, or the state's entire registry can be requested. Include a SASE (9" x 12" for the complete registry). There is no fee.

The state also plans to put its sex offender registry on the Internet. When available, find it through the Sexual Predator section at *www.crimetime.com*.

The City of Bangor maintains a telephone message line with offender names. Call 207-947-7382, then press *104. The recording ends with an invitation to view the city's registered sex offender book in person.

MAINE

OFFENDERS WHO MUST REGISTER

All persons sentenced on or after June 30, 1992 of Gross Sexual Assault when the victim was under 16 years of age. All persons sentenced after September 18, 1999 for any one of a number of sex-related or violent crimes.

Offenders sentenced between 6-30-92 and 9-17-99 must register for 15 years. Offenders sentenced after 9-17-99 must register for 10 years; sexually violent predators every 90 days for life.

OFFENDER PERSONAL IDENTIFIERS

Full Legal Name
Date of Birth
Address

AGENCY IN CHARGE

Maine State Police
State Bureau of Identification
36 Hospital Street
Augusta, ME 04330

Telephone: 207-624-7009

NOTES

Due to the inclusion only recently of many serious crimes which did not previously require registration, sole reliance on this information is not recommended. See chapter "How to Identify Unregistered Sex Offenders" for conducting a more in-depth criminal background check.

MARYLAND

INFORMATION AVAILABLE TO THE PUBLIC	The Maryland sex offender registry is open to the public. However, only limited information is available — it only includes persons convicted after October 1, 1995 and/or October 1, 1997. See below.

COMMUNITY SEARCH AVAILABLE?	Yes

NAME SEARCH AVAILABLE?	Yes

LEGAL AUTHORITY	Article 27, Section 792 Annotated Code of Maryland

EFFECTIVE DATE	October 1, 1995 (crimes with child victims) and October 1, 1997 (crimes with adult victims)

WHERE TO ACCESS INFO

Written requests for name checks and community checks can be made to the Department of Public Safety and Correctional Services (see address, facing page). The request must contain your name, address, phone number *and* reason for the request.

Local law enforcement agencies also maintain the registry on file for public inspection. Contact your local police or sheriff's station for details. In Prince George's County, information is available by phone. Call 301-985-3660.

Local law enforcement is also required to notify area schools when an offender is released.

MARYLAND

OFFENDERS WHO MUST REGISTER

Persons convicted after October 1, 1995 of certain sex offenses against children or after October 1, 1997 for certain sex offenses against adults.

Sex offenders must register for 10 years; sexually violent predators for life, or until relieved of the duty by a court.

OFFENDER PERSONAL IDENTIFIERS

Name
Aliases
Photograph
Address
Place of Employment
Date of Birth

AGENCY IN CHARGE

Dept. of Public Safety
Crimes Against Children &
Sex Offender Registry
P.O. Box 5743
Pikesville, MD 21282-5743

Telephone: 410-764-5160 ext. 314

NOTES

Persons convicted of serious crimes before October 1, 1995 will come up clean — a potentially dangerous shortcoming. See chapter "How to Identify Unregistered Sex Offenders" for information on running a statewide criminal check on a person in Maryland.

MASSACHUSETTS

INFORMATION AVAILABLE TO THE PUBLIC

After its original version of Megan's Law was struck down by the courts, a new law was passed in Massachusetts. It makes information on moderate and high-risk offenders available to the public. Look for a court challenge to this one, too.

COMMUNITY SEARCH AVAILABLE?	Yes
NAME SEARCH AVAILABLE?	Yes
LEGAL AUTHORITY	MGL Chapter 6, Section 178C
EFFECTIVE DATE	September 10, 1999

WHERE TO ACCESS INFO

Both name and community searches are available on a local level only. There is no public access to the statewide registry.

A seven-member board must conduct hearings for each of the state's estimated 13,000 potential registrants. Offenders will be graded as being low, moderate or high risk to re-offend. Low-risk offenders will be known to law enforcement only. Moderate and high-risk offenders will be identified to members of the public who inquire at a local police station. Law enforcement will proactively notify the community through flyers and other means when a high-risk offender is released.

As of our press date, Internet, phone or mail requests for offender information are not available.

MASSACHUSETTS

OFFENDERS WHO MUST REGISTER

Any offender who was convicted, or released from custody or parole, since October 1, 1981.

Offenders must register for 20 years after their release from supervision; sexual predators, for life.

OFFENDER PERSONAL IDENTIFIERS

Name
Photograph (if available)
Physical Description
Age
Home Address
Work Address

AGENCY IN CHARGE

Sex Offender Registry Board
200 Arlington Street
Chelsea, MA 02150

Telephone: 617-660-4600

NOTES

The new law also gives judges the power to sentence dangerous offenders to indefinite confinement at the Treatment Center for the Sexually Dangerous in Bridgewater.

MICHIGAN

INFORMATION AVAILABLE TO THE PUBLIC

The Michigan sex offender registry is open to the public. Its October 1, 1995 start date may warrant further investigation to identify older criminal charges. See chapter "How to Identify Unregistered Sex Offenders" for pre-1995 information.

COMMUNITY SEARCH AVAILABLE?	Yes

NAME SEARCH AVAILABLE?	No*

LEGAL AUTHORITY	Sex Offenders Registration Act

EFFECTIVE DATE	October 1, 1995

WHERE TO ACCESS INFO

On the Internet, the state's registry can be searched by zip code only. Access it through the Sexual Predator section at *www.crimetime.com* or directly at: *www.mipsor.state.mi.us/*.

*In 2000, look for name searches to become available over the Internet as well.

Local police agencies maintain information on locally registered offenders for public inspection.

Phone and mail requests for name or community searches are not available.

MICHIGAN

OFFENDERS WHO MUST REGISTER

Persons who were convicted, or were on probation, parole or incarcerated, on or after October 1, 1995.

First-time offenders must register for 25 years; repeat offenders, for life.

OFFENDER PERSONAL IDENTIFIERS

Name
Address
Physical Description
Date of Birth

AGENCY IN CHARGE

Michigan State Police
714 S. Harrison Road
East Lansing, MI 48823

Telephone: 517-336-6292

NOTES

Re-distributing information from the sex offender registry to any third party is a misdemeanor and, in addition, allows the person whose name was released to sue for damages.

MINNESOTA

INFORMATION AVAILABLE TO THE PUBLIC

Minnesota makes very little information available to the public from its sex offender registry. *Sole reliance on this limited information is not recommended.* See chapter, "How to Identify Unregistered Sex Offenders".

COMMUNITY SEARCH AVAILABLE?	No

NAME SEARCH AVAILABLE?	No

LEGAL AUTHORITY	Minn. Statute 244.052

EFFECTIVE DATE	January 1, 1997

WHERE TO ACCESS INFO

Local law enforcement is required to notify the community when a high-risk offender is released. When a moderate-risk offender is released, area schools, child care facilities and other groups may be notified. Only other law enforcement agencies will be notified upon the release of low-risk offenders.

Phone, mail and Internet information requests are not available.

MINNESOTA

OFFENDERS WHO MUST REGISTER

Sex offenders released after January 1, 1997 must register. Upon release a panel of experts rates the offender as low, moderate or high risk.

Offenders must register for 10 years.

OFFENDER PERSONAL IDENTIFIERS

Full Legal Name
Photograph
Date of Birth
Street and City of Residence
Physical Description

AGENCY IN CHARGE

Bureau of Criminal Apprehension
Attn.: Sex Offender Registry
1246 University Ave.
St. Paul, MN 55104

Telephone: 651-603-6748

NOTES

Fortunately, criminal history information is available in Minnesota. When checking on an individual, use statewide criminal history sources as found in the chapter "How to Identify Unregistered Sex Offenders".

MISSISSIPPI

INFORMATION AVAILABLE TO THE PUBLIC

The sex offender registry in Mississippi is open to the public. See details below.

COMMUNITY SEARCH AVAILABLE?	Yes*
NAME SEARCH AVAILABLE?	Yes
LEGAL AUTHORITY	MS Code Sec. 45-33-1
EFFECTIVE DATE	July 1, 1995

WHERE TO ACCESS INFO

Name checks can be conducted by mail only. Send $5 per name and a SASE to *Mississippi Department of Public Safety, Sex Offender Registry, P.O. Box 958, Jackson, MS 39205-0958.* The state has 14 days to respond.

*Local sheriff's departments maintain information on locally registered offenders. This information is open to the public and is the closest available thing to a community search.

Phone look ups and Internet searches are not available.

MISSISSIPPI

OFFENDERS WHO MUST REGISTER

Persons convicted of certain sex offenses. Applies retroactively to persons convicted prior to the law's effective date.

Offenders must register for 15 years, at which time they can apply to the courts for relief from registration.

OFFENDER PERSONAL IDENTIFIERS

Name
Address
Place of Employment

AGENCY IN CHARGE

Mississippi Dept. of Public Safety
Sex Offender Registry
P.O. Box 958
Jackson, MS 39205-0958

Telephone: 601-933-2600

NOTES

The state has been unable to pay its own way and has received a grant from the federal government to finance operation of its sex offender registry.

MISSOURI

INFORMATION AVAILABLE TO THE PUBLIC

The sex offender registry in Missouri is open to the public in limited form only. The entire state currently has 5,500 registrants. *Sole reliance on this restricted information is not recommended.* See chapter "How to Identify Unregistered Sex Offenders".

COMMUNITY SEARCH AVAILABLE?

Yes

NAME SEARCH AVAILABLE?

No

LEGAL AUTHORITY

Rev. Stat. Chap. 589 Sec. 400

EFFECTIVE DATE

January 1, 1995

WHERE TO ACCESS INFO

Police and sheriff departments maintain a list of locally registered offenders for public review. Local newspapers occasionally publish a list of locally registered offenders, too.

No Internet, phone or mail requests for offender information are presently available. Internet access may be available in the future.

MISSOURI

OFFENDERS WHO MUST REGISTER

Any person convicted of a felony sexual assault or child kidnapping since July 1, 1979.

Both sex offenders and sexual predators must register for life. Offenders must verify their address annually; sexual predators, every 90 days.

OFFENDER PERSONAL IDENTIFIERS

Name
Address

AGENCY IN CHARGE

Missouri State Highway Patrol
Criminal Records and Identification Division
1510 E. Elm Street
P.O. Box 568
Jefferson City, MO 65101

Telephone: 573-526-6153

NOTES

Luckily, Missouri has an open-record policy when it comes to obtaining someone's criminal history. If you're checking on a particular person, use a statewide criminal history search. See chapter "How to Identify Unregistered Sex Offenders".

MONTANA

COMMUNITY SEARCH AVAILABLE? Yes

NAME SEARCH AVAILABLE? Yes

LEGAL AUTHORITY Sexual or Violent Offender Registration Act

EFFECTIVE DATE July 1, 1989

WHERE TO ACCESS INFO

Name searches are available by phone or mail. A website is planned for the future.

To check a name by phone, call 406-444-9479 or 406-444-3875. There's no fee.

To check a name by mail, send your request to the Montana Department of Justice address on the opposite page. Free.

To conduct a community search, visit your local law enforcement agency where information on offenders registered in that particular jurisdiction can be viewed.

Local law enforcement agencies may also notify the news media when a high-risk offender is released into the community.

MONTANA

OFFENDERS WHO MUST REGISTER

Persons convicted, incarcerated or on probation or parole for certain sex offenses on or after July 1, 1989, or for certain violent offenses after October 1, 1995.

Offenders are required to register for life, but certain offenders can petition the courts for relief after 10 years if they do not have a second conviction.

OFFENDER PERSONAL IDENTIFIERS

Name*
Address*
Photo*
Date of Birth*

*Released at the discretion of local law enforcement officials.

AGENCY IN CHARGE

Montana Department of Justice
Div. of Criminal Investigation
P.O. Box 201417
Helena, MT 59620-1417

Telephone: 406-444-9479
or 406-444-3875

NOTES

The state's entire 2,000 plus name registry can also be purchased. Photocopying and handling fees apply.

NEBRASKA

INFORMATION AVAILABLE TO THE PUBLIC

Currently, Nebraska makes practically no information from its sex offender registry available to the public. Strong nominee for the worst implementation of Megan's Law in the country.

COMMUNITY SEARCH AVAILABLE?	No

NAME SEARCH AVAILABLE?	No

LEGAL AUTHORITY	Sex Offender Registration Act

EFFECTIVE DATE	January 1, 1997

WHERE TO ACCESS INFO

The Nebraska sex offender registry can be accessed by the Nebraska State Patrol only.

Supposedly, there can be notification of area schools, day care centers and communities when a high-risk offender is released. To date however, notifications have been far and few between.

NEBRASKA

OFFENDERS WHO MUST REGISTER

Offenders who were convicted after January 1, 1997, or were incarcerated, or on probation or parole as of this date.

Offenders must register for 10 years. Sexually violent offenders must register for 10 years, and then can apply for relief from registration.

OFFENDER PERSONAL IDENTIFIERS

Name
Address
Date of Birth

AGENCY IN CHARGE

Nebraska State Patrol
Attn.: Sex Offender Registry
P.O. Box 94907
Lincoln, NE 68509

Telephone: 402-471-4545

NOTES

Fortunately, Nebraska is a state where another person's statewide criminal history can be obtained. This will include all prior criminal convictions — sex-related and otherwise. See chapter "How to Identify Unregistered Sex Offenders".

135

NEVADA

INFORMATION AVAILABLE TO THE PUBLIC

Nevada now offers open public access to its sex offender registry, although community searches are not available.

COMMUNITY SEARCH AVAILABLE?	No

NAME SEARCH AVAILABLE?	Yes

LEGAL AUTHORITY	Statutes of NV 1997, Ch. 451

EFFECTIVE DATE	January 1, 1998

WHERE TO ACCESS INFO

Names can be checked by calling the Nevada Highway Patrol at 775-687-1600, extension 250. There's an $8 charge per name checked. (They'll bill you.) Results should come back the same day.

Name searches can also be done by mail at the Nevada Highway Patrol address on the facing page. Include $8 per name and a SASE or a telephone number. (They'll call you with the results.)

When sexual predators or other high-risk offenders are released, law enforcement may notify the community. For moderate-risk offenders, only schools and other child care organizations are notified. Only law enforcement is notified about the release of low-risk offenders.

NEVADA

OFFENDERS WHO MUST REGISTER

Persons convicted of any one of 20 sex-related crimes since July 1, 1956.

Registration is required for life, although after 15 years removal from registry can be applied for.

OFFENDER PERSONAL IDENTIFIERS

Name*
Photograph*
Date of Birth*
Social Security Number*
Home and Work Street Location*
Vehicle Description*

For Tier 3 (high risk) offenders. Less information is released on Tier 1 and 2 offenders.

AGENCY IN CHARGE

Nevada Highway Patrol
Records & Identification Services
808 W. Nye Lane
Carson City, NV 89703

Telephone: 775-687-1600 ext. 250

NOTES

Law enforcement community notification efforts may include release of information to the news media as well as going door-to-door with flyers containing offender information.

NEW HAMPSHIRE

INFORMATION AVAILABLE TO THE PUBLIC

Limited information is available to the public. Only the names of offenders whose victims were under age 13, 17 or 18 (depending on the crime) are public record — this is roughly 17% of the state's total registered sex offender population. The rest are known to law enforcement only.

COMMUNITY SEARCH AVAILABLE?	Yes*
NAME SEARCH AVAILABLE?	Yes*
LEGAL AUTHORITY	RSA 651B
EFFECTIVE DATE	January 1, 1999

WHERE TO ACCESS INFO

Local police stations maintain files on locally registered offenders. The file is public record, but a form must be filled out and identification shown prior to viewing.

*Community and name searches are of limited value as they only include offenders whose victims were under 13, 17 or 18 years of age, depending on the crime committed.

TV station WMUR has independently obtained the state's list of publicly identified offenders and posted them on the Internet at *www.wmur.com*.

NEW HAMPSHIRE

OFFENDERS WHO MUST REGISTER

Any offender convicted of certain sex offenses who, depending on the crime, was incarcerated, on parole, on probation or convicted on or after January 1, 1988 or January 1, 1996.

Offenders must register for 10 years; serious offenders, for life.

OFFENDER PERSONAL IDENTIFIERS

Name
Address
Date of Birth

AGENCY IN CHARGE

New Hampshire State Patrol
Attn.: Special Investigations Unit
10 Hazen Drive
Concord, NH 03305

Telephone: 603-271-2663

NOTES

New Hampshire has a patchwork system in place. *Sole reliance on this information is not recommended.* See chapter "How to Identify Unregistered Sex Offenders" to bypass these flaws.

NEW JERSEY

INFORMATION AVAILABLE TO THE PUBLIC

Ironically, New Jersey, the state that gave birth to Megan's Law, has one of the nation's weakest programs. Neither name nor community searches are available.

COMMUNITY SEARCH AVAILABLE?	No
NAME SEARCH AVAILABLE?	No
LEGAL AUTHORITY	Megan's Law
EFFECTIVE DATE	October 31, 1994

WHERE TO ACCESS INFO

Local law enforcement can notify the community when Tier 3 and 2 (high and moderate-risk) offenders are released. The released information becomes public record and can be repeated elsewhere, including in local newspapers. To date there have been 350 community notifications.

Schools and other youth organizations may be notified when a moderate-risk offender is released. When Tier 1 (low risk) offenders are released, only the victim and law enforcement agencies are notified.

There is no Internet, phone or mail access to offender information.

NEW JERSEY

OFFENDERS WHO MUST REGISTER

Any person convicted since October 31, 1994 of certain sex offenses or any person diagnosed since 1976 as being a "repetitive and compulsive" offender.

Offenders must register annually for 15 years, at which point they can then apply for relief from registration.

OFFENDER PERSONAL IDENTIFIERS

Name
Address
Photograph

AGENCY IN CHARGE

NJ Division of Criminal Justice
P.O. Box 085
Trenton, NJ 08625

Telephone: 609-984-2814

NOTES

Sole reliance on this restricted information is not recommended. See chapter "How to Identify Unregistered Sex Offenders" for obtaining criminal history information, if any, on a particular person.

141

NEW MEXICO

INFORMATION AVAILABLE TO THE PUBLIC

New Mexico makes virtually no information available to the public due to a late starting date for their program — it only includes sex offenders convicted after July 1, 1999.

COMMUNITY SEARCH AVAILABLE?

Yes

NAME SEARCH AVAILABLE?

Yes

LEGAL AUTHORITY

Sex Offender Registration and Notification Act

EFFECTIVE DATE

July 1, 1999

WHERE TO ACCESS INFO

Name searches can be conducted by calling the New Mexico Department of Public Safety at 505-827-9181.

Name or community searches can also be obtained by sending a written request to the DPS address on the opposite page. Community searches are broken down by county. There's a fee of $1 per page.

Look for a website to go up in the year 2000. When available, find it via the Sexual Predator section at *www.crimetime.com.*

NEW MEXICO

OFFENDERS WHO MUST REGISTER

Any offender who was convicted of certain sex offenses after July 1, 1999. *WARNING: Persons convicted before this date will not show up in a check of the registry.*

All offenders must register for life.

OFFENDER PERSONAL IDENTIFIERS

Full Legal Name
Home Address
Place of Employment
Date of Birth

AGENCY IN CHARGE

New Mexico Dept. of Public Safety
Attn.: Sex Offender Registry
P.O. Box 1628
Santa Fe, NM 87504-1628

Telephone: 505-827-9181

NOTES

WARNING: Due to the late starting date of this program, both name and community searches should not be relied upon. For alternatives, see chapter "How to Identify Unregistered Sex Offenders".

143

NEW YORK

INFORMATION AVAILABLE TO THE PUBLIC

New York's sex offender registry is open to the public in limited form. Name lookups are available; meaningful community searches are not. *Sole reliance on this information is not recommended.*

COMMUNITY SEARCH AVAILABLE?	No

NAME SEARCH AVAILABLE?	Yes

LEGAL AUTHORITY	The N.Y. State Sex Offender Registration Act

EFFECTIVE DATE	January 21, 1996

WHERE TO ACCESS INFO

Name searches of the state's nearly 9,500 registered sex offenders can be made at 1-900-288-3838. There's a charge of $5 per name checked and the caller must provide the person's name and at least one personal identifier. Call 8 a.m. to 5 p.m., Monday through Friday.

A statewide sub-directory of sexual predators is distributed semi-annually to local police agencies for public viewing.

Neither mail nor Internet look ups are available.

144

NEW YORK

OFFENDERS WHO MUST REGISTER

Any offender who was convicted, on probation or on parole on or after January 21, 1996.

Level 1 and 2 offenders must register for 10 years, level 3 for life.

OFFENDER PERSONAL IDENTIFIERS

Name
Address
Photograph

AGENCY IN CHARGE

New York State Division of Criminal Justice Services
Attn.: Sex Offender Registry Unit
4 Tower Place
Stuyvesant Plaza
Albany, NY 12203

Telephone: 518-457-6326

NOTES

Sole reliance on the New York sex offender registry is not recommended due to the January 21, 1996 start date. Pre-1996 registration information may be unreliable. For alternatives, see chapter "How to Identify Unregistered Sex Offenders".

NORTH CAROLINA

INFORMATION AVAILABLE TO THE PUBLIC

North Carolina offers one of the most open sex offender registries in the nation. However, it has one shortcoming: It only contains names of offenders convicted on or after January 1, 1996. See "Notes" section on opposite page.

COMMUNITY SEARCH AVAILABLE?	Yes

NAME SEARCH AVAILABLE?	Yes

LEGAL AUTHORITY	Amy Jackson Law

EFFECTIVE DATE	January 1, 1998

WHERE TO ACCESS INFO

On the Internet, the statewide registry can be searched by name, city, county or zip code. Find it at the Sexual Predator section at *www.crimetime.com* or directly at *http://sbi.jus.state.nc.us/sor*.

The sheriff in each county also maintains a registry of offenders registered locally. This can be viewed by the public. By submitting a written request, a member of the public can obtain a copy of the entire county's registry.

A copy of the state's entire sex offender registry can be requested by contacting the agency in charge. (See box, opposite page.)

No phone or mail-in requests for offender information are available.

NORTH CAROLINA

OFFENDERS WHO MUST REGISTER

Persons convicted on or after January 1, 1996 of certain sex offenses and/or child kidnapping/abduction or felonious restraint when the perpetrator is not the child's parent.

Offenders must register for 10 years, sexual predators, indefinitely, but can apply for relief from registration after ten years.

OFFENDER PERSONAL IDENTIFIERS

Full Legal Name
Aliases
Date of Birth
Physical Description
Address
Photograph

AGENCY IN CHARGE

North Carolina
State Bureau of Investigations
Division of Criminal Information
407 N. Blount Street
Raleigh, NC 27601

Telephone: 919-733-3171

NOTES

Due to the January 1, 1996 start date, sole reliance on this information is not recommended. A person convicted prior to this time would come up clean. See chapter "How to Identify Unregistered Sex Offenders" for additional options.

NORTH DAKOTA

North Dakota has two different sex offender registries. The smaller, official one (which complies with Megan's Law) allows for public notification of the community only when a high-risk offender is released. The second, called the *Non-Registrant List*, is larger and is wholly available upon request.

COMMUNITY SEARCH AVAILABLE?
No

NAME SEARCH AVAILABLE?
Yes

LEGAL AUTHORITY
N.D. Cent. Code 12.1-32-15

EFFECTIVE DATE
August 1, 1995

WHERE TO ACCESS INFO

The official Megan's Law list, which complies with federal guidelines, cannot be accessed for name or community searches. However, law enforcement can make community notifications if a risk is present.

The Non-Registrant List can be requested in whole or single name checks can be obtained by sending a written request to the ND Bureau of Criminal Investigation (see address on opposite page).

Telephone look ups and Internet searches are not available.

OFFENDERS WHO MUST REGISTER

Both the Megan's Law list (now with over 780 names) and the Non-Registrant List (1,058 names) include offenders convicted or incarcerated on or after August 1, 1985.

Offenders must register for 10 years.

OFFENDER PERSONAL IDENTIFIERS

Full Legal Name*
Photograph*
Address*
Date of Birth*

*When community notifications are made for high risk offenders.

AGENCY IN CHARGE

North Dakota Bureau of Criminal Investigation
P.O. Box 1054-A
Bismarck, ND 58502

Telephone: 701-328-5500

NOTES

The Non-Registrant List consists of names extracted from the state's Criminal Record History System. Address information on offenders may be out-of-date as registration is not required. Out of state offenders who move to ND will *not* be found here, either. Advice: Check this Non-Registrant List and stay alert for community notifications from the official Megan's Law list.

OHIO

INFORMATION AVAILABLE TO THE PUBLIC

Currently, Ohio offers limited information to the public from its sex offender registry. County-level checks are available, but statewide ones are not. See details below.

COMMUNITY SEARCH AVAILABLE?	Yes

NAME SEARCH AVAILABLE?	No

LEGAL AUTHORITY	Ohio Revised Code 2950.01

EFFECTIVE DATE	July 1, 1997

WHERE TO ACCESS INFO

Statewide name checks of the Ohio sex offender registry are not available to the public, but information on offenders registered in any given county is public record. Go to your nearest sheriff's office.

The sheriff departments in three counties (Summit, Greene, Stark) have posted their Sexual Predators (High Risk) and Habitual Sexual Offenders (Medium Risk) on the Internet. Visit the Sexual Predator section at *www.crimetime.com* for links to these local registries.

Law enforcement agencies should notify the next-door neighbors when high or medium-risk offenders are present. The surrounding neighborhood and community may *not* be notified. Local school boards, child care centers, institutions of higher learning and others are also notified.

OHIO

OFFENDERS WHO MUST REGISTER

Any offender who was incarcerated as of July 1, 1997, or who was convicted on or after July 1, 1997, or who was required to register under the prior sex offender registration law.

Sexual Predators must register for life; Habitual Sex Offenders for 20 years; all others, for 10 years.

OFFENDER PERSONAL IDENTIFIERS

Full Legal Name*
Photos*
Age*
Address*
Physical Description*

*At the discretion of local law enforcement.

AGENCY IN CHARGE

Ohio Attorney General
Attn.: S.O.R.N.
Box 1580
State Route 56
London, OH 43140

Telephone: 614-466-8204 x224

NOTES

Ohio's failure to allow access to its statewide registry makes it possible for offenders to slip through the cracks. When doing a background check on an individual, obtaining further information is advisable. See chapter "How to Identify Unregistered Sex Offenders".

OKLAHOMA

INFORMATION AVAILABLE TO THE PUBLIC

The Oklahoma sex offender registry is now open to the public, although disbursement of the information to the public is somewhat inconvenient.

COMMUNITY SEARCH AVAILABLE?	Yes
NAME SEARCH AVAILABLE?	Yes
LEGAL AUTHORITY	Sex Offenders Registration Act
EFFECTIVE DATE	July 1, 1995

WHERE TO ACCESS INFO

The entire statewide registry can be viewed (but not copied) at the Oklahoma Department of Corrections in Oklahoma City. Name searches can be done by mail here, too. *Free.* (See address, facing page.)

Police and sheriff departments maintain information on locally registered offenders which is available for public viewing. Copies are available to schools and other child care organizations.

Local law enforcement has great leeway in making community notifications. Some police departments, such as the Tulsa PD, release the information to newspapers for publication.

Phone and Internet searches are not available.

OKLAHOMA

OFFENDERS WHO MUST REGISTER

Offenders who were convicted on or after November 1, 1989 must register as sex offenders. An offender who receives a second conviction after November 1, 1997 is to be designated as a sexual predator.

Sex offenders must register for ten years, sexual predators for life.

OFFENDER PERSONAL IDENTIFIERS

Full Legal Name
Address
Photograph
Date of Birth
Vehicle Description

AGENCY IN CHARGE

Oklahoma Dept. of Corrections
Attn.: Sex Offender Registry
3400 Martin Luther King Ave.
Oklahoma City, OK 73136

Telephone: 405-425-2872

NOTES

For possible pre-1989 convictions on any given person, use techniques described in chapter "How to Identify Unregistered Sex Offenders".

OREGON

INFORMATION AVAILABLE TO THE PUBLIC

Oregon's sex offender registry is open to the public, with access through several different means. See details below.

COMMUNITY SEARCH AVAILABLE?	Yes
NAME SEARCH AVAILABLE?	Yes
LEGAL AUTHORITY	O.R.S. 181.585 - 181.589
EFFECTIVE DATE	September 1, 1999

WHERE TO ACCESS INFO

Single names can be checked by phone. Call the Oregon State Police at 503-378-3720 and ask for Sex Offender Registration. Community searches can also be requested by phone, but the results will be mailed back. *Free.*

Name or community searches can also be requested by mail. Send your request to the OSP address on the opposite page. *Free.*

The Oregon State Police or other law enforcement agencies may proactively notify the community with flyers and press releases when a high-risk offender is present.

A website is planned but is currently under legal challenge.

OREGON

OFFENDERS WHO MUST REGISTER

Offenders who were incarcerated or convicted on or after October 3, 1989 for certain sex offenses.

All offenders must register for life, although after 10 years they can apply for relief from registration.

OFFENDER PERSONAL IDENTIFIERS

Name
Photograph
Address
Date of Birth
Physical Description

AGENCY IN CHARGE

Oregon State Police
Attn.: Sex Offender Reg. Unit
Public Service Building, Rm 400
Salem, OR 97310

Telephone: 503-378-3720

NOTES

The state currently has over 8,000 registrants.

Be sure to use personal identifiers to properly identify offenders.

PENNSYLVANIA

INFORMATION AVAILABLE TO THE PUBLIC

Pennsylvania offers a very, very limited Megan's Law. *Reliance on this information is strongly not recommended.* Rather, conduct a criminal background check as described in chapter "How to Identify Unregistered Sex Offenders".

COMMUNITY SEARCH AVAILABLE?	No
NAME SEARCH AVAILABLE?	No
LEGAL AUTHORITY	42 Pa. Cons. Stat. §§ 9791 et seq.
EFFECTIVE DATE	January 21, 1996

WHERE TO ACCESS INFO

The statewide sex offender registry is available to law enforcement only. A subsection of the main database, sexually violent predators, is available to the public. However, it only applies to offenders who committed their crimes on or after April 21, 1996. See "Notes" section, opposite page.

Local police are authorized to release information on locally registered sexually violent predators. They are also required to notify neighbors, local school superintendents, child care facilities and institutions of higher learning.

There is no Internet, phone or mail-in request available.

PENNSYLVANIA

OFFENDERS WHO MUST REGISTER

Offenders who were convicted, incarcerated, on probation or on parole on or after January 21, 1996.

Offenders must register for 10 years; sexually violent predators must register for life, unless relieved of the duty by a court.

OFFENDER PERSONAL IDENTIFIERS

Name
Photograph
Address

AGENCY IN CHARGE

Pennsylvania State Police
Attn.: Megan's Law Unit
1800 Elmerton Ave.
Harrisburg, PA 17110

Telephone: 717-783-4363

NOTES

As we go to press, a court ruling has further weakened the state's already poor implementation of Megan's Law. You'll want to sidestep the whole mess in Pennsylvania and conduct a criminal background check on the person you are investigating. Fortunately, statewide criminal histories can be obtained on another person in this state.

RHODE ISLAND

INFORMATION AVAILABLE TO THE PUBLIC

Sharply limited Megan's Law information is available to the public in Rhode Island. Very, very little protection is offered to the public through the state's program.

COMMUNITY SEARCH AVAILABLE?	No

NAME SEARCH AVAILABLE?	No

LEGAL AUTHORITY	R.I. Gen. Laws §§ 11-37.1-1 et seq.

EFFECTIVE DATE	July 24, 1996

WHERE TO ACCESS INFO

Phone, mail, or Internet look ups of offender information are not available. Only law enforcement can access the state's sex offender registry.

Local law enforcement may notify at-risk persons in the community upon the release of moderate and high-risk offenders.

RHODE ISLAND

OFFENDERS WHO MUST REGISTER

Persons convicted of certain sex crimes who were convicted or incarcerated on or after July 1, 1992. Also includes persons who committed additional Megan's Law offenses, such as child kidnapping by a non-parent, when the crime was committed on or after July 24, 1996. Offenders must register for 10 years; sexually violent predators for life.

OFFENDER PERSONAL IDENTIFIERS

Full Legal Name
Photograph
Physical Description
Date of Birth
Approximate Address

AGENCY IN CHARGE

Rhode Island Attorney General
150 S. Main Street
Providence, RI 02903

Telephone: 401-274-4400

NOTES

For conducting an in-depth background investigation on a particular person, see chapter "How to Identify Unregistered Sex Offenders". Community searches are not available here.

SOUTH CAROLINA

INFORMATION AVAILABLE TO THE PUBLIC

South Carolina's sex offender registry is open to the public via both the Internet and local sheriff stations. See details below.

COMMUNITY SEARCH AVAILABLE?	Yes
NAME SEARCH AVAILABLE?	Yes
LEGAL AUTHORITY	Sex Offender Registry
EFFECTIVE DATE	January 1, 1995

WHERE TO ACCESS INFO

On the Internet, the state's sex offender registry can be searched by offender name, city, county or zip code. Information returned includes offender photograph, name, and address. Find it at *www.crimetime.com* or directly at *www.scattorneygeneral.com/public/registry.html*.

Local sheriff stations also maintain information on locally registered offenders, including photographs.

Community notifications are not made in South Carolina. Mail and phone inquiries not available.

SOUTH CAROLINA

OFFENDERS WHO MUST REGISTER

Any person convicted or released from prison after January 1, 1995 for certain sex offenses. Includes juvenile offenders as young as 12 years of age.

Offenders must register for life.

OFFENDER PERSONAL IDENTIFIERS

Full Legal Name
Photograph
Date of Birth
Sex
Race
Address

AGENCY IN CHARGE

S.C. Law Enforcement Division
Attn.: Sex Offender Registry
P.O. Box 21398
Columbia, SC 29221

Telephone: 803-896-7051

NOTES

The 1995 start date of the South Carolina registry makes overreliance on it unwise. Persons convicted before this date may not show up in a check of the registry. Statewide criminal histories, covering all years, are available in South Carolina. See chapter "How to Identify Unregistered Sex Offenders".

161

SOUTH DAKOTA

INFORMATION AVAILABLE TO THE PUBLIC

The South Dakota sex offender registry is open to the public in limited fashion. A statewide check of the registry is not available. County-level checks can be done.

COMMUNITY SEARCH AVAILABLE?	Yes
NAME SEARCH AVAILABLE?	Yes
LEGAL AUTHORITY	S.D. Cod. Laws §§ 22-22-30 etc.
EFFECTIVE DATE	July 1, 1994

WHERE TO ACCESS INFO

Local law enforcement agencies maintain information on offenders registered in that county. This information is public record.

Unfortunately, the statewide registry is available to law enforcement only.

There is no Internet, mail-in or telephone access to the registry.

SOUTH DAKOTA

OFFENDERS WHO MUST REGISTER

Includes persons who were convicted of felony sex crimes prior to the law's effective date.

Offenders must register for life, but can apply for relief from registration.

OFFENDER PERSONAL IDENTIFIERS

Name*
Address*
Photograph*
Date of Birth*

Released at the discretion of local law enforcement agencies.

AGENCY IN CHARGE

South Dakota Division of Criminal Investigations
Attn.: Sex Offender Registry
East Highway 34
c/o 500 E. Capitol Ave.
Pierre, SD 57501-5070

Telephone: 605-773-3331

NOTES

Since a statewide check of the state's registry is not possible, further efforts may be warranted when checking on the background of another person. See chapter "How to Identify Unregistered Sex Offenders".

163

TENNESSEE

INFORMATION AVAILABLE TO THE PUBLIC

Although Tennessee has passed its own version of Megan's Law, the entire program has been hobbled by a court ruling which prevents the release of any information to the public about the state's sex offender population.

COMMUNITY SEARCH AVAILABLE?	No
NAME SEARCH AVAILABLE?	No
LEGAL AUTHORITY	Sexual Offender Registration and Monitoring Act
EFFECTIVE DATE	July 1, 1995

WHERE TO ACCESS INFO

Currently, the state's sex offender registry cannot be accessed due to a ruling preventing release of information to the public by the Federal District Court for the Middle District of Tennessee. Look for either a Supreme Court challenge or passage of new legislation in the future. For future updates, visit the Tennessee Bureau of Investigation homepage, located at:

www.tbi.state.tn.us

Police agencies continue to have access to the registry for law enforcement purposes.

TENNESSEE

OFFENDERS WHO MUST REGISTER

Offenders convicted, incarcerated, on probation or on parole for certain sex offenses on or after January 1, 1995.

Offenders must register for life, but can apply for relief from registration after then years.

OFFENDER PERSONAL IDENTIFIERS

None available at this time.

AGENCY IN CHARGE

Tennessee Bureau of Investigation
Attn.: Criminal Intelligence Div.
1148 Foster Ave.
Nashville, TN 37210

Telephone: 615-741-0430
(toll free) 1-888-837-4170

NOTES

Until the legal situation is resolved in Tennesse, use the techniques described in "How to Identify Unregistered Sex Offenders".

The state currently has 3,600 plus registered offenders.

TEXAS

WHERE TO ACCESS INFO

On the Internet, the registry can be searched by a person's name, city or zip code. Photographs and full street addresses of registered offenders are withheld from the public. Sex offender registry searches on the Internet are free. Find it through the Sexual Predator section at *www.crimetime.com* or directly at *http://records.txpds.state.tx.us/dps/so_search.cfm.*

Names can also be checked by mail. Send $10.00 per name to the address on the facing page. Be sure to include all available personal identifiers.

Local law enforcement agencies shall notify the community by media releases when an offender with a prior child victim is released. They also maintain information on locally registered offenders for public viewing.

Telephone look ups are not available.

TEXAS

OFFENDERS WHO MUST REGISTER

Persons, including juveniles, convicted of certain sex offenses who were incarcerated or under supervision on or after September 1, 1997 for crimes committed after September 1, 1970.

Offenders must register for 10 years, sexually violent predators for life.

OFFENDER PERSONAL IDENTIFIERS

Name
Photograph
Address
Physical Description
Date of Birth

AGENCY IN CHARGE

Crime Records Service
Texas Dept. of Public Safety
P.O. Box 4143
Austin, TX 78765-4143

Telephone: 512-424-2479

NOTES

Texas has an admirable Megan's Law program. Unfortunately, though, it only includes persons who were incarcerated or under supervision on or after September 1, 1997. *This is a potentially serious loophole.* Advice: Use this, but expand your search and obtain a statewide criminal history on the person you are investigating. This will identify all past convictions — sex-related and otherwise — prior to the 1997 date.

UTAH

INFORMATION AVAILABLE TO THE PUBLIC

The Utah sex offender registry is available to the public in limited form. Currently, information is available only on registered sex offenders convicted after April 29, 1996.

COMMUNITY SEARCH AVAILABLE?	Yes

NAME SEARCH AVAILABLE?	Yes

LEGAL AUTHORITY	UT Annotated Code § 77-27-21.5

EFFECTIVE DATE	April 29, 1996

WHERE TO ACCESS INFO

On the Internet, a search can be run by zip code, city, or offender name. Only offenders convicted after April 29, 1996 are included, though. Access it via the Sexual Predator section at *www.crimetime.com* or directly at *www.cr.ex.state.us/soreg/home.htm?*

For those without Internet access, a written request can be made to the address in the "Agency in Charge" box. Name and community searches can be requested. You can also request a list of offenders in your zip code plus one neighboring zip code. All written requests must include the requester's name, address and phone number.

168

UTAH

OFFENDERS WHO MUST REGISTER

Offenders convicted of certain sexual offenses after April 29, 1996.

All offenders must register for 10 years.

OFFENDER PERSONAL IDENTIFIERS

Name
Age
Address
Physical Description
Vehicle
Photograph

Only partial information is available through the Internet. Total information is available by mail.

AGENCY IN CHARGE

Utah Department of Corrections
Sex Offenders Registry Program
6100 South Fashion Blvd., Rm 100
Murray, UT 84107

Telephone: 801-265-5500

NOTES

The April 29, 1996 start date makes sole reliance on Utah's Megan's Law unwise. Persons convicted of crimes before this date will go undetected. See chapter "How to Identify Unregistered Sex Offenders" for other options.

VERMONT

INFORMATION AVAILABLE TO THE PUBLIC

Vermont has a very restrictive Megan's Law, offering little information to the public. Checks of the statewide registry are not possible. See details below.

COMMUNITY SEARCH AVAILABLE?	No

NAME SEARCH AVAILABLE?	Yes

LEGAL AUTHORITY	Vt. Sex Offender Registration Act

EFFECTIVE DATE	July 1, 1996

WHERE TO ACCESS INFO

Access to the statewide sex offender registry is not available to the public. However, the public may visit local police stations to conduct a name search of locally registered offenders *only*. *WARNING: If the offender being checked is not registered or is registered in another jurisdiction, he will come up clean.* Further, state law provides that local law enforcement agencies *may* release the information, not *shall*.

Community searches are not available.

Law enforcement does not conduct community notifications in Vermont.

VERMONT

OFFENDERS WHO MUST REGISTER

Offenders convicted of certain sex offenses who were under the supervision of the Department of Corrections as of July 1, 1996 or were convicted after this date.

Offenders must register for 10 years; sexual predators for 10 years, when they can then petition for relief from registration.

OFFENDER PERSONAL IDENTIFIERS

Name
Address
Date of Birth
Physical Description

AGENCY IN CHARGE

Vt. Criminal Information Center
103 S. Main Street
Waterbury, VT 05671

Telephone: 802-244-8727

NOTES

Advice: Use this weak system, but also consider further investigation into the background of the person you are investigating by using the techniques described in chapter "How to Identify Unregistered Sex Offenders".

VIRGINIA

INFORMATION AVAILABLE TO THE PUBLIC	Virginia's sex offender registry is open to the public. The state's registered sex offender population is divided into two groups: Sexually Violent Offenders and Sex Offenders. The former is searchable on the Internet only, the latter by mail only.

COMMUNITY SEARCH AVAILABLE?	Yes

NAME SEARCH AVAILABLE?	Yes

LEGAL AUTHORITY	Sex Offender and Crimes Against Minors Registry

EFFECTIVE DATE	July 1, 1997

WHERE TO ACCESS INFO

On the Internet, visit the Virginia State Police website where information is available on nearly 6,000 sexually violent offenders. *The website does NOT include regular sex offenders.* Searchable by name, zip code, county or city. Find it via *www.crimetime.com* or at directly at *http://sexoffender.vsp. state.va.us/cool-ICE.*

Also at the VSP website, schools, other child care organizations and foster homes can register to receive electronic notification about locally registered sex offenders and sexually violent offenders.

By mail, name searches can be conducted of the regular sex offenders. Cost is $15. Form 266 must be used. Obtain it at any law enforcement agency or on the Internet at *www.vsp.state.va.us* by clicking the State Police Forms button.

Phone look ups are not available.

VIRGINIA

OFFENDERS WHO MUST REGISTER

Offenders convicted, incarcerated or on probation or parole on or after July 1, 1994 for certain sex offenses.

Sex offenders must register for 10 years, sexually violent offenders for life.

OFFENDER PERSONAL IDENTIFIERS

Name
Photo
Sex
Race
Physical Description
Home Address
Work Address

AGENCY IN CHARGE

Virginia State Police
Attn.: Sex Offender Registry
P.O. Box 27472
Richmond, VA 23261

Telephone: 804-674-2147

NOTES

The Sexually Violent Offender database has 6,000 names, the Sex Offender database has 2,000.

Consider running a criminal background check here to identify older, pre-1994 convictions. See chapter "How to Identify Unregistered Sex Offenders".

WASHINGTON

Washington's sex offender registry is open to the public — for those who know how to access information through the state's public disclosure law. See details below.

COMMUNITY SEARCH AVAILABLE?	Yes
STATEWIDE NAME SEARCH AVAILABLE?	Yes
LEGAL AUTHORITY	WA Revised Code § 4.24.550 etc.
EFFECTIVE DATE	1996

WHERE TO ACCESS INFO

The state's entire sex offender registry can be obtained in totality in only one way: by contacting the Public Records Office of the Washington State Patrol. Upon written request, the entire registry, some 15,000 names, will be sent to you on diskette. It's updated monthly. First-time users must sign a declaration that the information will be used for non-commercial purposes. Send your request to *Washington State Patrol, Attn.: Public Records Office, P.O. Box 42600, Olympia, WA 98504*; 360-753-5966. *Free.*

On the Internet, a few cities and counties have posted information on locally registered offenders. Find these sites via the Sexual Predator section at *www. crimetime.com.*

Local law enforcement may notify the community when moderate and high-risk offenders are released. This includes postings at local sheriff's offices.

WASHINGTON

OFFENDERS WHO MUST REGISTER

Offenders convicted of certain sex offenses who were in custody, or on probation or parole, on or after July 28, 1991.

Depending on seriousness of their crime, offenders must register for ten or fifteen years, or until relieved of the duty by a court.

OFFENDER PERSONAL IDENTIFIERS

Name
Photograph
Approximate Address
Date of Birth

AGENCY IN CHARGE

Washington State Patrol
Attn.: Criminal History & Identification
P.O. Box 42633
Olympia, WA 98504

Telephone: 360-705-5100

NOTES

If you need to check on the criminal conviction history of a person before 1991, consider obtaining the person's statewide criminal history. This is available to the public in Washington and can be obtained by mail or over the Internet. See chapter "How to Identify Unregistered Sex Offenders" for full details.

WEST VIRGINIA

INFORMATION AVAILABLE TO THE PUBLIC

West Virginia makes public some of its statewide sex offender registry. The identity of the worst offenders are made public. Less serious offenders are not public record.

COMMUNITY SEARCH AVAILABLE?	Yes

NAME SEARCH AVAILABLE?	Yes

LEGAL AUTHORITY	Sex Offender Registration Act

EFFECTIVE DATE	June 13, 1999

WHERE TO ACCESS INFO

The West Virginia State Police will release information on locally registered offenders to the county superintendent of schools and to community or religious organizations.

The state's registry is being posted on the Internet at the rate of one county per month. As of our press date, 11 of 55 counties were online. *Only lifetime registrants are included in Internet postings; less serious offenders will not be identified here.* Both name and community searches can be done for the counties online. Access them via *www.crimetime.com* or directly at *http://www.wvstatepolice.com/sexoff/sexoff.shtml.*

Offender information is not available by phone or mail.

176

WEST VIRGINIA

OFFENDERS WHO MUST REGISTER

Offenders convicted of certain sex offenses retroactive to the effective date of the law. Their records go back decades.

Offenders must register for 10 years. If the victim was a minor, or the offense was violent, or the offender is a repeat offender, lifetime registration is required.

OFFENDER PERSONAL IDENTIFIERS

Full Legal Name
Photograph
Date of Birth
Physical Description

AGENCY IN CHARGE

West Virginia State Police
Attn.: Sex Offender Registry
725 Jefferson Road
South Charleston, WV 25309

Telephone: 304-746-2133

NOTES

The state's policy of withholding information on less serious offenders makes sole reliance on the registry unwise. Advice: Use their public information but also conduct a name search for unregistered sex offenders — see page 185.

177

WISCONSIN

The Wisconsin sex offender registry is open to the public, with dissemination through a toll-free telephone hotline and other avenues. Overall, an excellent program.

COMMUNITY SEARCH AVAILABLE?	Yes
NAME SEARCH AVAILABLE?	Yes
LEGAL AUTHORITY	Wisconsin Act 440
EFFECTIVE DATE	June 1, 1997

WHERE TO ACCESS INFO

Wisconsin offers a state-of-the-art telephone information line for name checks. If the name you are checking is found, you'll need one of these identifiers to confirm the information: date of birth, Social Security Number, or driver's license number. Call anytime: 1-800-398-2403. *Free.*

Names can be checked by mail. Form *Registry Public Inquiry* should be used. It's available from local law enforcement agencies and from the Wisconsin DOC. Call them at 608-266-3831 to have a blank form faxed or mailed. *Free.*

Community searches are also available. Names of offenders registered in a specific geographic area will be released to bonafide neighborhood watch groups, who are then free to openly disseminate the information. Start by obtaining a *Neighborhood Watch Request for Information Form* from your local law enforcement agency.

WISCONSIN

OFFENDERS WHO MUST REGISTER

Offenders convicted of certain sex offenses who were incarcerated or on probation or parole, on or after December 25, 1993.

Offenders must register for 15 years; repeat offenders, for life.

OFFENDER PERSONAL IDENTIFIERS

Full Legal Name
Photo
Date of Birth
Address
Physical Description
Vehicle Description

Information released may vary depending on agency and risk of offender.

AGENCY IN CHARGE

Department of Corrections
Attn.: S.O.R.P.
149 E. Wilson
Madison, WI 53707

Telephone: 608-266-3831
Name Searches: 1-800-398-2403

NOTES

Local police agencies may also notify the community about high-risk offenders. Several cities, including Madison and Milwaukee, have posted highest-risk offenders on the Internet. Access these via the Sexual Predator section at *www.crimetime.com.*

WYOMING

The Wyoming sex offender registry is open to the public in limited form via community notifications and a website limited to high-risk offenders.

COMMUNITY SEARCH AVAILABLE?	No
NAME SEARCH AVAILABLE?	No
LEGAL AUTHORITY	Stat. §§ 7-19-301 et seq.
EFFECTIVE DATE	July 1, 1999

WHERE TO ACCESS INFO

As we go to press, Wyoming's program is in a state of transition, coming into compliance with the federal Megan's Law.

By early 2000, a website should be up with information on high risk offenders. When it's available, access it through the Sexual Predator section at *www. crimetime.com.* Telephone, mail or other requests for offender information are not available.

Law enforcement agencies are authorized to notify neighbors who live within 750 feet of moderate and high-risk offenders.

WYOMING

OFFENDERS WHO MUST REGISTER

Persons convicted of certain sex offenses committed after January 1, 1985. A court hearing must take place to designate offenders as moderate or high risk, subjecting them to possible community notification.

Offenders must register for 10 years; sexual predators for life.

OFFENDER PERSONAL IDENTIFIERS

Name
Aliases
Photograph
Address
Date of Birth
Place of Birth
Physical Description

AGENCY IN CHARGE

Division of Criminal Investigation
Attn.: WSOR
316 W. 22nd Street
Cheyenne, WY 82002-0001

Telephone: 307-777-7181

NOTES

Unfortunately, information on low and moderate-risk offenders is not widely disseminated. To learn more about the criminal background of a particular person, see chapter "How to Identify Unregistered Sex Offenders".

How to Identify unRegistered SEX Offenders

How to Identify Unregistered Sex Offenders

In Pennsylvania, the names of regular sex offenders are not made public, and only the names of the more serious "sexually violent predators" who were convicted on or after April 21, 1996 are publicly available. And, as we go to press, even this limited release of information is being legally challenged. Obviously, if you're in a state like Pennsylvania, you're not going to want to put your safety into the hands of a Megan's Law that is narrow in scope and offers little protection. You'll want to take matters into your own hands and determine if a given person is an *unregistered* sex offender.

An *unregistered sex offender* is a person who has been arrested and convicted of a sex-related crime, but has not been required to officially register as a *registered sex offender* in the state where he lives because of Megan's Law limitations. Nevertheless, he still has a history of criminal convictions — and you can find out all about them — if you know where to look.

There are two primary methods for determining if a person is an unregistered sex offender. The first is by running a statewide criminal history on the person. Currently, this option is available in 43 states. If you're from a state where statewide criminal checks are *not* available, you'll want to proceed to plan B, which is to conduct research at local criminal courts.

There are two other things you should know about searching for unregistered sex offenders. First, you'll be learning not only about the person's prior convictions for sex-related offenses, but in fact about all of his or her past criminal convictions. The second thing you should know is a potential flaw in this method: If the offender was convicted of a crime in another state, his conviction will not be uncovered by your investigation. If you know what state the person previously resided in, then obviously, you'll want to conduct a background check there as well.

WARNING!

Conducting a statewide or local criminal check to determine if a person has been previously convicted of sex or other of-fenses will NOT identify crimes committed in another state!

Conducting Statewide Criminal Histories

As with conducting a name search for a registered sex offender, you'll want to begin by arming yourself with as much information about the person you are investigating as possible. At the least, you should have the person's full legal name and date of birth. In most cases, this will also be all that you'll need. Don't have either of these? You'll need to backtrack to the chapter "Obtaining Personal Identifiers" and do some basic detective work.

On the following pages you'll find my exclusive *Guide to Statewide Criminal Checks*. It's the end result of over two and a half years of seeking out sources of information within the criminal justice system that are lawfully available to non-law enforcement persons. This information is your key to obtaining statewide criminal histories *without* the permission of the person being investigated. In several states the information is available — but only with the signed consent of the person being investigated. For obvious reasons, we'll regard these states as not making statewide criminal histories available.

You'll note that there are two basic places we obtain

these statewide criminal histories from. The first is through state criminal history repositories. Many states let you access another person's criminal history upon request, and by paying a nominal fee. However, many states do not let you obtain another person's statewide criminal history, restricting this information to law enforcement agencies, unless a signed consent form is obtained from the person being investigated. In addition, a set of fingerprints may also be required. For our purposes, neither of these options is very practical — we'll work around them.

There's a second, insiders' way to get essentially the same information in those states that don't allow access to statewide criminal records. Ironically, many of these states *will* allow access to their state prison inmate histories. For example, in California, statewide criminal histories are not available to the general public. However, by simply calling the right phone number at the Department of Corrections, you can learn if a person has been incarcerated in state prison! Throughout the United States, incarceration in a state prison invariably means that there has been a felony conviction. However, you should also know that sometimes felony convictions can result in either probation or local jail time. In these latter two cases, such an outcome would *not* be detected by state prison inmate history checks.

The
Guide to
Statewide
Criminal Checks

ALABAMA

Statewide criminal histories are maintained by the Alabama Bureau of Investigation. They're available to the public only with the signed consent of the person being investigated.

The Alabama Department of Corrections makes information on previously incarcerated felons available to the public. By phone, a name check can be done for felons released within the past five years. Call 334-240-9550.

The same prison history information, but going back ten years or more, can be obtained by mailing a written request. There's no fee, but a SASE should be included. Send to: *Alabama Department of Corrections, Attn.: Central Records Office, P.O. Box 301501, Montgomery, AL 36130.*

ALASKA

The Alaska Department of Public Safety maintains the state's criminal records repository. Statewide criminal records are not open to the public.

The Alaska Department of Corrections' official policy is that incarceration history information on previously held persons is *not* public record.

For information on inmates currently incarcerated in the state's prison system, call the Jail Access Information Line (JAIL) to learn charges, bail information, scheduled parole hearings and more. The cost is $1.25 for the first minute and 95¢ for each additional minute. Call 1-900-226-5040.

ARIZONA

Arizona is a closed-record state — statewide criminal histories are not available to the public.

The Arizona Department of Corrections' Offender Services Bureau has information on previously incarcerated persons going back to 1986. Call 602-542-5586. When the automated attendant provides choices, select the *Public Access* option.

Also available from the Arizona DOC is its *Inmate Information Line*, a pay-per-call service for information on currently held inmates. Operates 24 hours a day. Cost is $1.25 for the first minute and 95¢ for each additional minute. Call 1-900-226-8682.

ARKANSAS

Statewide criminal checks are not available in Arkansas without the signed consent of the person being investigated.

However, the Arkansas Department of Corrections will release information on previously convicted felons who were incarcerated from the mid-1980's through the present. There's no fee, but inquiries must be mailed. Include a SASE along with the name and DOB of the person being checked to: *Arkansas Department of Corrections, Attn.: Diagnostics Unit, 7500 Correction Circle, Pine Bluff, AR 71603.*

CALIFORNIA

In California, statewide criminal checks are limited to law enforcement only unless the person being investigated gives his or her signed consent. Other requirements also apply.

However, there is a legal, backdoor way to access much of the same information. By calling the California Department of Corrections with a person's name and DOB, you can learn if he or she has a history of incarceration in the state's prison system since 1977. The line is operated 24 hours a day, 7 days a week. Call 916-445-6713.

STATEWIDE CRIMINAL CHECKS

COLORADO

Colorado makes rap sheets (arrests and convictions) available to the public. This is one of the few states where arrest information (when there is not necessarily a following conviction) can be obtained. You'll need to pay a $7 fee per name checked and complete a form called *Public Request for Information*. Call the Colorado Bureau of Investigation Information Line for details at 303-239-4680.

The Colorado Department of Corrections will release information on persons previously incarcerated in its state prison system. Their records span from 1976 through the present. You'll need a name and DOB to conduct a name check. Call the Colorado DOC at 719-579-9580 and ask for Records.

CONNECTICUT

Connecticut offers statewide criminal conviction histories for $25 per name. Their data goes back to the 1960's. Turnaround time is approximately two weeks. Includes both felony and misdemeanor convictions. Send your request including the fee, name and DOB of the person being checked to *Connecticut Department of Public Safety, Bureau of Identification, P.O. Box 2794, Middleton, CT 06457*. Checks should be made payable to "The Commissioner of Public Safety". Requests are filled by mail only. For further information, call 860-685-8480.

In addition, the Connecticut Department of Corrections keeps track of persons who were previously incarcerated in the state's prison system. They'll do name look ups by phone when provided with a name and DOB. Their computerized data goes back to the 1980's. Call 860-692-7480.

DELAWARE

Neither statewide criminal histories nor prison history checks are available in Delaware.

DISTRICT OF COLUMBIA

District of Columbia criminal checks can be done through the *DC Superior Court* by telephone. Includes felony and some misdemeanor convictions since 1978. Have the subject's name and DOB ready when you call. Telephone: 202-879-1373.

FLORIDA

Florida allows criminal history checks without the permission of the person being investigated. The cost is $15 per name. Requests should be made on the state's *Criminal History Information Request* form. The form can be found on the Internet at *www.fdle.state.fl.us.* Then click the Criminal History Info button. The form can also be requested by sending a SASE to *Florida Department of Law Enforcement, USB/Public Records, P.O. Box 1489, Tallahassee, FL 32302*; 850-410-8109.

On the Internet, information on currently incarcerated persons can be obtained at the Florida Department of Corrections' *Inmate Population Information Search* form. Find it at *www. dc.state.fl.us/inmateinfomenu.asp.*

GEORGIA

Although Georgia doesn't have a statewide criminal check available to non-law-enforcement parties, the Georgia Department of Corrections will release information on any person who has previously been incarcerated in a state prison. Their database goes back decades. To conduct a name search by telephone, call Inmate Information at 404-656-4569. Be ready to provide the name, race and DOB of the person.

The state will also release information about a person who is under active parole supervision. Call the Georgia Board of Pardons & Parole, 404-656-5330.

HAWAII

Hawaii will release a person's adult criminal history, including both felonies and misdemeanors. Send the person's name, DOB and SSN plus a $15 fee. (They prefer payment by money order or cashier's check.) Send your request to *Department of Attorney General, Hawaii Criminal Justice Data Center, Room 101, 465 S. King Street, Honolulu, HI 96813*; 808-587-3106.

The Hawaii Department of Public Safety's Inmate Classification Department maintains information on persons who have been incarcerated in state prison going back to the 1960's. They can search by name or Social Security Number, but both are preferred. Date of birth is also helpful. Here are three direct numbers into Inmate Classification: 808-587-1337; 808-587-1336; and 808-587-2566.

IDAHO

Idaho will not release a person's criminal history without the signed consent of the person whose name is being checked.

However, the Idaho Department of Corrections will release information on convicted felons who have served time in a state penal institution. Their database goes back to 1979. In addition to the person's name, also be prepared to provide a DOB and SSN. The information is provided by phone. Call 208-658-2000 and ask for Records.

ILLINOIS

Statewide criminal histories are available to law enforcement only in Illinois.

The Illinois Department of Corrections will release information on previously incarcerated felons, going back to the early 1990's. The information can be accessed by phone or over the Internet. By phone, call 217-522-2666 and ask for extension 2008. Online, go to *www.idoc.state.il.us*. The website contains an option to look up by Social Security Number as well. If a hit is found, substantial background information is returned on the offender.

INDIANA

The Indiana State Police maintain statewide criminal records in Indiana. They are available to law enforcement only and to employers who complete State Form 8053. Call 317-232-8262 for the form and further details.

However, the Indiana Department of Corrections will release information by phone on persons who have been incarcerated in a state prison going back to the middle of 1989. The main switchboard number for the Indiana Department of Corrections is 317-232-5715. When the automated attendant answers, try hitting option 1, then option 2. Or, better yet, try these direct lines into the Records Department: 317-232-5716; 317-232-5765; 317-232-5772.

IOWA

Iowa will release the adult criminal conviction history of a subject, including both felonies and serious misdemeanors.

Arrest information without a disposition will also be included for the past 18 months. The fee is $13 per name checked. Your request must be made on a special state-provided form. If you want a person checked under two names (e.g., a married name and maiden name), two fees and two request forms must be submitted. The forms and further instructions can be obtained by calling this number and asking for a *Non-Law-Enforcement Record Check Request* form and a *Billing* form. They'll fax you what you need. The same form can also be obtained over the Internet at *www.state.ia.us/government/dps/dci*. Call 515-281-5138 for further details.

The Iowa Department of Corrections will also release information on previously incarcerated felons. Their data goes back at least 20 years. Information is available by phone. Call 515-281-4811.

KANSAS

In Kansas, statewide criminal histories are available to the public. A user agreement, called the *Criminal History Record Request and Agreement*, must be requested from the Kansas Bureau of Investigation. After executing the agreement, names can be checked for $10 each. Turnaround time is eight to ten weeks. Call 785-296-8200. Look for this information to be available over the Internet starting in the year 2000. Find details at *www.kbi.state.ks.us.*

A much easier avenue is to telephone the Kansas Department of Corrections. Adult felony conviction information which resulted in state prison incarceration is public record in Kansas. Their database includes persons incarcerated from 1978 to the present. Call the Records Department directly at 785-296-0521.

KENTUCKY

Kentucky is one of the few states with a centralized collection of criminal court conviction records. The person whose record is being checked is notified, however. The name checks are done by mail only. Cost is $10 each and they take a week to fulfill. Call 502-573-2350, ask for Records, and then request to be faxed a *Record Request Form*.

The Kentucky D.O.C. will release information on previously incarcerated felons. Their records go back to the early 1980's. Call Offender Information directly at 502-564-2433.

LOUISIANA

The Louisiana State Police maintain the state's repository of criminal records. However, this information is available to the public only with the signed release of the person being investigated. Call 225-925-6095 for further details.

The Louisiana Department of Corrections maintains a database going back to the 1980's of previously incarcerated persons. Call 225-319-4223 to run a name.

MAINE

Maine offers adult criminal conviction histories to anyone requesting the information. The state's criminal records aren't computerized yet, so there's a slow turnaround time — possibly three months. Send $7.00, the subject's name and date of birth, to *Maine State Police, Bureau of Identification, 3600 Hospital Street, Augusta, ME 04330;* 207-624-7009.

The Maine Department of Corrections will release information on persons incarcerated going back to 1959. You'll need the person's name and DOB. The direct line for doing a name check is 207-287-4381. If this is busy, try the main switchboard at 207-287-2711 and tell the operator you need to check if a person was previously incarcerated.

MARYLAND

The primary source for statewide criminal records in Maryland is the state's Criminal Justice Information System (CJIS). The CJIS will report all misdemeanor and most felony criminal charges filed statewide. (Felony charges filed directly by prosecutors, usually as a result of a grand jury indictment, may not be reported.) The system is open only to qualified subscribers. Single searches are not available directly from CJIS. Call 888-795-0011 for details. In short, this is an option for private investigation agencies but not the public.

However, if you're in need of just an occasional CJIS look up, you can contact Maryland-based Business Research and Intelligence, Inc. They take credit cards and will do CJIS look ups for $15 per name. They can search CJIS using a name only; but a DOB is necessary for positive identification. Call them at 301-390-8768.

The Maryland Department of Corrections' Data Processing Unit will release information on previously incarcerated persons. They need a name and DOB to do the search. Results are available by phone. Their data goes back 20 years. Here are two direct lines to the unit: 410-585-3351; 410-585-3352.

MASSACHUSETTS

Massachusetts is another state that's on the books as offering a statewide criminal history. Look at the details, though, and you'll realize it's all but worthless. In short, the state will tell you if a person's had a felony conviction — but only if they've completed their sentence, probation or parole within the last three years. A convicted murderer who completed his sentence and parole more than three years ago would come up clean! Call 617-660-4600 for further details.

The Massachusetts Department of Corrections doesn't release information on past or present inmates to the public.

MICHIGAN

Statewide criminal records are available to the public in Michigan on a mail-in basis. Information returned will be all felony and misdemeanor convictions going back to the 1950's. Send a letter and $5 per name to the Michigan State Police requesting a "Criminal History Record". Include the full name, DOB, race and sex of the person being investigated. If available, also include the person's Social Security Number and Michigan driver's license number. There's a two-to-three-week turnaround time. Mail your request to: *Michigan State Police, Central Records Division, 7150 Harris Drive, Lansing, MI 48913;* 517-322-1955.

The Michigan D.O.C. maintains a database of previously incarcerated persons going back to the mid-1950's. They'll do a look up over the phone if provided with the person's full legal name and either a DOB or SSN. Call 517-373-0284.

The Michigan Department of Corrections also maintains a website with public access to its Offender Tracking Information System (OTIS). It's a database of offenders incarcerated after July 1, 1995. Find it online at *www.state.mi.us/mdoc/asp/ otis1.html.*

MINNESOTA

Minnesota will release felony and certain misdemeanor conviction information without the permission of the person being investigated. Record checks are not done by phone. Public record information released will be for the last 15 years only. Send the subject's full name and DOB with a SASE to *Bureau of Criminal Apprehension, 1246 University Ave, St. Paul, MN 55104.* Include a fee of $4 per name checked. Indicate that you are requesting a *Public Record Criminal History Check.* Payment accepted by money order, company check or personal check. Call 651-642-0670 for further details.

Information on persons previously incarcerated by the Minnesota Department of Corrections is available by phone. Their information goes back over 20 years. Call Records at 651-642-0322. Information on currently incarcerated prisoners can also be obtained on the Internet at the Minnesota Department of Corrections' website, *www.doc.state.mn.us/publicviewer/.*

MISSISSIPPI

Neither statewide criminal histories nor inmate history information are available in Mississippi.

MISSOURI

Missouri statewide criminal record checks are available without the subject's consent. Send a check or money order for $5 per name to *Missouri State Highway Patrol, Attn: Criminal Records, P.O. Box 568, Jefferson City, MO 65102.* Include the subject's name, DOB and SSN. All convictions, pending charges, and a 30-day arrest history will be released. Records date back to the 1960's. Call 573-526-6153 for further information.

Also in Missouri, the Department of Corrections maintains publicly available information on previously incarcerated persons going back decades. There's no charge and the results are given by phone. Have the person's name, DOB and SSN available when calling. Inquiries are handled by the Probation and Parole Department, 573-751-8488.

MONTANA

Montana will provide criminal history information. Included are felony criminal convictions going back to the subject's 18th birthday, plus misdemeanor convictions for the past five years. Turnaround time is seven to ten days. Fee is $5 per name checked. Include the subject's name, any known aliases, DOB, SSN and SASE. Phone checks not done. Mail request to: *Montana Department of Justice, Identification Bureau, 303 N. Roberts, #374, Helena, MT 59620;* 406-444-3625.

The Montana Department of Corrections maintains information on persons incarcerated in state prisons going back to 1978. The information is public record. Contact the Montana DOC Records Department directly at 406-444-9521.

NEBRASKA

Nebraska allows criminal history checks without the consent of the subject. Records returned include all arrests and convictions when the arrestee's fingerprints have been taken. In practical terms, this means felonies and serious misdemeanors. There's a 15-day turnaround time. Fee is $10 per name checked. Send the fee and the person's name, DOB, SSN and any aliases to *Nebraska State Patrol, Attn: CID, P.O. Box 94907, Lincoln, NE 68509-4907;* 402-471-4545.

The Nebraska Department of Correctional Services maintains information on all persons who have been incarcerated in state penal institutions at any time going back to mid-1977. They'll do a name check by phone. The direct line for the Records Department is 402-479-5661. If the line is busy, try the main switchboard at 402-471-2654 and ask for Records.

NEVADA

The Nevada Highway Patrol maintains the state's criminal record repository. However, information will be released only if they are provided with both the signed consent of the person being investigated and a set of his or her fingerprints.

The Nevada Department of Corrections will release information on persons previously incarcerated in state prison. Their records go back many decades. In addition to the person's name, they also prefer to have a SSN and/or DOB. Turnaround time for information is very quick. They prefer inquiries to be faxed to 775-687-6715. If no fax machine is available, call them directly at 775-887-3285 and tell the operator you want to check a name to see if a person was previously incarcerated.

NEW HAMPSHIRE

Statewide criminal histories are released in New Hampshire only with the signed consent of the subject of the investigation.

However, the state's Department of Corrections' Offender Records section will release information on persons previously or currently incarcerated. Their computer name check, which can be done by phone, goes back to 1994. Manual checks of prior years are also available if requested. They'll release information on the person's crime and the sentence received. Call 603-271-1823.

NEW JERSEY

The New Jersey State Police maintain statewide criminal records. They're not available to the public.

The New Jersey Department of Corrections' Inmate Locator line is very hard to get through on. However, when you finally bust through the busy signals, you can learn if a person was previously incarcerated in state prison going back to 1976. Call 609-777-5753.

Also of interest in New Jersey are postings on the Internet of Parole Eligibility Notices by the State Parole Board. Find it online at *www.state.nj.us/parole/elig.htm.*

NEW MEXICO

The New Mexico Department of Public Safety maintains statewide criminal record histories. Information is released only with the signed consent of the person being investigated.

The New Mexico Department of Corrections will tell you if a person has been incarcerated in a state prison at any time in the last 25 years. Call 505-827-8709 and ask for Records. They'll provide results over the phone; be prepared to provide the name of the person being checked and as many personal identifiers as possible.

NEW YORK

Statewide criminal records are not available to the public in the state of New York without a court order.

The New York City area maintains a somewhat centralized search system called the *Unified Court System,* with 13 counties included. However, they can only search one county at a time. (The counties are Bronx, Dutchess, Erie, Kings, Nassau, New York, Orange, Putnam, Queens, Richmond, Rockland, Suffolk, and Westchester.) Cost is $16 per name per county. Name checks return information on convictions and pending prosecutions and can be conducted by mail-in or walk-in request. Name searches by phone are not available. Turnaround time is one to two business days. Requests must be submitted on their Criminal History Record Search (CHRS) form. Call 212-428-2810 to request a CHRS form and further instructions. They'll fax it to you if asked nicely.

The New York State Department of Correctional Services maintains a database of currently and previously incarcerated persons going back 25 years. After release, a convict will remain in the system for a minimum of 15 years. The information is available by phone at 518-457-5000 or on the web at *www.docs.state.ny.us.* Once at the page, scroll down to the "inmate lookup" link to be taken to the search page.

Also worthy of note in the state of New York is the Victim Information and Notification Everyday (VINE) system. The system allows crime victims and members of the public to obtain information on the release date of currently incarcerated inmates. You'll need the inmate's name and DOB *or* his Department of Corrections Identification Number (DIN) *or* his New York State Identification Number (NYSID) which can be obtained by calling the prosecuting district attorney's office. Your call must be made from a touch-tone phone. Call 888-846-3469.

NORTH CAROLINA

Statewide criminal histories are not available to the public in North Carolina.

However, the North Carolina Department of Corrections maintains a database of previously incarcerated persons going back to 1974. It's open to the public and they'll do a name search over the phone. Call the Combined Records unit at 919-716-3200. They can also search their records by Social Security Number.

In addition, the North Carolina Department of Corrections' website contains additional searchable databases. The Inmate Releases file contains state prison system parolees who were released since January 1, 1998. A second searchable database, Public Access Information System, contains information on inmates incarcerated since July 1, 1995. Both can be accessed at *www.doc.state.nc.us.*

Also coming soon to North Carolina will be the state's implementation of SAVAN (Statewide Automated Victim Assistance & Notification), which will allow crime victims to obtain up-to-date information on offenders by calling 1-877-NCSAVAN.

NORTH DAKOTA

North Dakota will release a person's statewide history for felony and some misdemeanor convictions. Also included are certain events from the preceding 12 months, including arrests. Call 701-328-5500 and request a *Non-Criminal Justice Records Release Form*. After completing the form, return it with a $20 fee to the North Dakota Bureau of Criminal Investigation. (Note: The person whose name is checked is notified by the state that his or her criminal history has been requested. However, the identity of the requester is kept confidential.)

The North Dakota Department of Correction and Rehabilitation keeps track of persons incarcerated in state prison going back to 1965. They'll do a name check by phone. Call Inmate Records directly at 701-328-6125. If the line is busy, try the central office at 701-328-6390 and ask for Inmate Records.

OHIO

Statewide criminal records are available in Ohio only with the signed consent of the person being investigated. A set of fingerprints from the person being investigated is also required.

Ohio Professional Electronic Network (OPEN) offers a computerized database of county arrest records from 82 of Ohio's 88 counties. The data comes from jail bookings — if the arrestee wasn't booked into jail, there will be no record. Some of the information goes as far back as 1967. The information is available online, on a subscription basis. This is one of the very few databases of arrest records (as opposed to conviction records) publicly available anywhere. Call 800-366-0106 or 614-481-6980.

If you'd like to access the OPEN database of Ohio arrest records on an as-needed basis without subscribing, you can contact Ohio private investigation agency, FYI Investigations at 614-890-1330. They accept credit cards and will do a search of the Ohio arrest record database for a flat fee of $25 per name.

The Ohio Department of Rehabilitation and Correction maintains information on previously incarcerated persons going back to the 1970's. The only persons not included are "hideaways" who have been extracted from the system for reasons including witness protection. Preferred search criteria are a name and SSN, but a DOB is also useful. Call the Records Retention Center directly at 614-752-1073. The same information is available on the Internet at *www.drc.ohio.gov/cfdocs/inmate/search.htm*.

OKLAHOMA

Oklahoma has an open criminal record policy. For a fee of $15 per name, the Oklahoma State Bureau of Investigation (OSBI) will conduct a statewide criminal arrest history. Their records go back to 1925 and include any person who was arrested *and* fingerprinted. Oklahoma is one of the few states that release arrest (as opposed to conviction only) information. The searches are available by mail or fax. To request an OSBI statewide criminal check by mail, send a letter stating the reason for the request, the subject's full legal name, any aliases, race, sex, DOB and SSN and a SASE. The fee of $15 per name checked must be paid by business check or money order only. Personal checks are not accepted. Turnaround time for mail requests is approximately two weeks. Mail to: *Oklahoma State Bureau of Investigation, Criminal History Reporting, 6600 North Harvey, Building 6, Suite 140, Oklahoma City, OK 73116*; 405-848-6724.

OSBI searches can also be done by fax using a credit card. Turnaround time for fax/credit card requests is approximately two days. Call 405-848-6724, ask for Records, and then ask that a blank fax search form be faxed to you.

The Oklahoma Department of Corrections maintains records on previously incarcerated persons going back to approximately 1984. The information is available to the public. Call

Records directly at 405-425-2624 to run a name check. If this line is busy, call the Oklahoma DOC main switchboard at 405-425-2500 and ask for Records.

OREGON

Oregon statewide criminal histories are available without the subject's consent — but there's one catch: The subject of the inquiry is sent a letter and told that you have requested his or her criminal history. Felony and misdemeanor conviction information going back to the subject's 18th birthday is included. Limit requests to one name per letter and include the person's name, DOB and last known address. Send payment in the amount of $15 per name to *Oregon State Police, Attn: Open Records, Unit 11, P.O. Box 4395, Portland, OR 97208*; 503-378-3070.

The Oregon Department of Corrections will run a name check by phone to determine if a person was previously incarcerated in the state prison system. Their computerized records cover 1983 through the present. Call 503-945-0920.

PENNSYLVANIA

The Pennsylvania State Police offers felony conviction data from its central repository. The information is available by mail or over the Internet after registration has been completed. No consent is necessary from the person being investigated. There is a $10 fee per name searched. To do a search by mail, you'll need to use their form, *Request for Criminal Record Check*. To obtain the form, call 717-783-5494 and ask that it be mailed or faxed to you. Complete the form and mail back with a $10 fee per name checked. To check the status on submitted forms, call 717-783-9222.

The information can also now be obtained on the Net. However, a registration form must be completed and a user name and password issued. The Pennsylvania Access to Criminal History (PATCH) system can be found at *http://patch.state.pa.us/psp/Overview.htm*.

The Pennsylvania Department of Correction's Inmate Records unit will release information on persons previously incarcerated. Their records go back to at least the 1970's. You'll need a name and at least one personal identifier to do a name check. Call Inmate Records directly at 717-730-2721.

RHODE ISLAND

Statewide criminal histories are available only with the signed consent of the person being investigated.

The Rhode Island Department of Corrections maintains a database of persons who have been incarcerated since 1992. They'll conduct a name check by phone. Call the Records Department directly at 401-462-3900.

SOUTH CAROLINA

South Carolina will release criminal conviction information from all years and arrest information that is less than one year old. There's a seven-to-ten-day turnaround. Send payment in the amount of $25 per name checked, payable by money order or company check *only*. Include the subject's name, DOB and SSN (if available). Also include a SASE. Mail request to: *South Carolina Law Enforcement Division, Attn: Records, P.O. Box 21398, Columbia, SC 29221*; 803-737-9000.

The South Carolina Department of Corrections will do a name check by phone to determine if a person was previously incarcerated. Goes back to the 1970's. Call 803-896-8531.

SOUTH DAKOTA

Statewide criminal histories can be obtained only with the signed consent of the person being investigated.

The South Dakota Department of Corrections maintains a database of currently and past prisoners, going back approximately ten years. The information is available to the public and they'll do a name check by phone. Call 605-773-3478.

TENNESSEE

Statewide criminal records are off limits to the public in Tennessee.

However, the Tennessee Department of Corrections' Sentence Information unit will provide information on previously incarcerated persons. Their computerized records go back to February of 1992. However, a manual search of earlier records is available upon request. You'll need both a name and DOB to run a check. Call the unit directly at 615-741-2773.

Persons who were placed on parole or probation in other states but who are residing in Tennessee can be identified at the Tennessee Internet Crime Information Center website, located at *www.ticic.state.tn.us* or by calling 1-888-837-4170.

TEXAS

Texas statewide criminal histories are now available thanks to a new public records act that took effect September 1, 1997. A person's misdemeanor and felony conviction criminal history and/or felony deferral record will be released without his or her consent. Send a $10 fee, plus as many identifiers as possible on the subject, including name, DOB, SSN, race and sex. Requests are currently turned around in about 48 hours. Send your request to *Texas Department of Public Safety, Attn: Crime Records Service, P.O. Box 15999, Austin, TX 78761-5999*; 512-424-2474.

The same information can also be found on the state's website and the cost is $3.15 per name. However, be forewarned that the website can be frustrating — it's poorly designed and plagued by technical troubles. Find it here: *http://records.txdps.state.tx.us/dps/default.cfm.*

But wait...there's an even better way to check statewide criminal records in Texas. A private firm called Quick Search has the same information and will run a name for $7.00. Credit card payment accepted by phone. Call 214-358-2840.

The Texas Department of Corrections (TDC) won't do phone checks but they will search their records if a mail-in request is received. Their records go back to the 1850's. The service is free, but takes approximately two weeks to complete. Send your request including the subject's name and either DOB or TDC number and a SASE to: *Inmate Records, Texas Department of Corrections, P.O. Box 99, Huntsville, TX 77340*; 409-294-6509.

UTAH

In Utah, statewide criminal records are not public record.

Records on currently incarcerated persons and those on probation or parole are public information. However, persons previously incarcerated and no longer or probation or parole will not be indicated. Call the Utah State Department of Corrections, 801-265-5500.

VERMONT

Statewide criminal records can be obtained in Vermont only with the signed consent of the person being investigated. Other restrictions also apply. Call 802-244-8727 for further details.

Incarceration histories are not public record in Vermont.

VIRGINIA

Statewide criminal histories are maintained by the Virginia State Police and are available only with the signed consent of the person being investigated. Other requirements also apply.

The Virginia Department of Corrections will check their records to determine if a person was previously incarcerated. Their records go back to the 1980's. The requester must have the person's full name and DOB. Call 804-674-3209. If this line is busy, try the main switchboard at 804-674-3000 and ask for Inmate Intake.

Virginia has broken new ground with a program that releases information on offenders who are currently under parole supervision. (It's known informally as the Know Thy Neighbor Law.) For a fee of $5 any person can request a printout of all persons on parole within a given zip code. For $37.50, you can receive a similar list (on paper or computer disk) for the entire state. For 24-hour information, call 804-674-3243. To obtain the list, mail your payment and request to: *Virginia Department of Corrections, Attn: Victim Services Unit, 6900 Atmore Dr, Richmond, VA 23225.*

WASHINGTON

In the state of Washington, statewide criminal conviction histories are public record. Information returned includes criminal convictions; arrests from the past year when there is no disposition; and whether the person is a registered sex offender or kidnapper. The information is available both by mail and over the Internet.

To request a criminal check by mail, you'll need to obtain Form 3000-240-569 (also known as *Request for Conviction Criminal History Record*) by calling the Washington State Patrol at 360-705-5100. Ask for Customer Service — they can either fax or mail the form to you. After the form has been completed, return it with a $10 fee per name to: *Identification and Criminal History Section, Washington State Patrol, P.O. Box 42633, Olympia, WA 98504-2633.* Turnaround time for mail requests is approximately 7 to 14 working days.

The same information is available over the Internet with a credit card. Results are instantaneous. The fee is still $10 per name. The online system, known as WATCH (Washington Access to Criminal History) can be found at *http:// watch.wsp.wa.gov/WATCHOPEN/default.asp.*

The Washington D.O.C. has information on persons incarcerated going back to the 1970's. They'll do a name check by phone. They prefer the caller to have the name, DOB and SSN of the person being checked. Call 360-753-6454.

WEST VIRGINIA

The West Virginia State Police maintain the state's criminal record repository. However, statewide criminal histories are available only with the signed consent of the person being investigated. Other requirements also apply. Call 304-746-2100 for further details.

The West Virginia Division of Corrections will conduct a name check by phone to determine if a person has been previously incarcerated. Their computerized records go back five years; their master card index system goes back decades. Call 304-558-2037, and select extension 40 or 42 to be connected to Records.

WISCONSIN

Wisconsin arrest and conviction information from 1971 through the present is available without the subject's consent. Required information is the subject's name, DOB, sex, and race. Send a SASE, and payment in the amount of $13 per name checked. Mail your request to: *Crime Information Bureau, Attn: Record Check Unit, P.O. Box 2688, Madison, WI 53701-2688*; 608-266-5764.

In addition, the Wisconsin Department of Corrections makes incarceration history information available by phone. Their records go back to 1962. Records between 1962 and 1982 contain minimal information. Records since 1982 contain details such as charges and length of incarceration. To check a name, call the Master Record Check unit directly at 608-266-2097.

WYOMING

Statewide criminal records are available in Wyoming only with the signed consent and fingerprints of the person being checked. Prison name checks are not available in the state, either.

Using
Courthouse Records

If you're conducting an investigation in a state that doesn't allow access to statewide criminal records, you'll want to use the next best thing — criminal court records. In practical terms, you'll probably need this section only if you're in one of the following states: *Delaware, Massachusetts, Utah, Vermont or Wyoming.* These are the states that have either a weak or fledgling Megan's Law *and* don't allow the public to freely access another person's statewide criminal history.

The information you'll obtain from a courthouse criminal record check is basically the same information you would obtain from a statewide criminal check, but at a local level. The obvious shortcoming of this method is that you'll have to check each individual jurisdiction (usually county-level) where the person being investigated previously lived — potentially a large task if the person has been transient. Further, if the person was arrested and convicted in a jurisdiction away from home, this may go undetected by your criminal court check. These shortcomings make using courthouse records your last resort for checking into someone's background. Your first resort should be your state's sex offender registry as allowable under

Megan's Law. If this is not available or is incomplete, you'll next want to try a statewide criminal record check. If this isn't available in your state, you'll want to proceed to a criminal court check as described in this chapter.

Inside Criminal Court Files

Anytime a person is arrested, tried and convicted in a criminal court in the United States, a record is created which is open to the public. The only exceptions to this are the relatively rare situations when a court file is sealed or expunged. You'll be accessing these records to learn about the criminal history, if any, of any given person.

What can be found inside a criminal court file? Usually quite a bit, including most of the following:

• A *Criminal Complaint,* which lays out the charges against the arrestee.

• A *Police Report,* which may lay out all of the salacious details of the matter in graphic detail. (Note: Police reports are not public record in all areas.)

213

• *Trial transcripts,* which will indicate who said what during testimony as well as *trial minutes,* which are a summary of what occurred during the proceedings on a given date.

• A *disposition sheet or "dispo",* which shows the outcome of the charges. Usually this will be one of the following: Guilty, Not Guilty, Dismissed or Plea of No Contest.

• A *sentencing sheet* which shows the details of the sentence, probation or fine received by a convicted party.

• A *probation report,* which may contain information about the person's prior arrests and/or convictions.

Depending on the individual court and the seriousness of the crime, these criminal files may be kept in archives indefinitely. In Los Angeles, my home turf, criminal court archives go all the way back to the Old West days.

Now let me give you a quick lesson in how to search criminal court records to learn if a given person has any cases on file there. By "search" I don't necessarily mean in person. What I'm about to describe to you can many times be done by phone or mail.

WARNING!

As with sex offender registries, positive identification of a person's criminal record can be made only by matching two or more of the following personal identifiers:

Full Legal Name
Date of Birth
Social Security Number
Last Known Address
Photograph/Mug Shot

Failure to match two or more personal identifiers between the person you are investigating and a criminal court record may result in identifying a criminal history with the wrong person.

The Three-Steps for Researching Criminal Court Records

A brief overview should be helpful before getting immersed in the details of conducting a courthouse criminal check. Essentially we'll need to accomplish three basic tasks to check someone's past record of criminal convictions through courthouse records.

Step One:
Find the Right Courthouse

Finding the right courthouse to check in will be our first step. This will involve a telephone call or two to directory assistance, assuming that you already know the jurisdiction that you want to check in. If you don't, further efforts will be necessary. More on this later.

Step Two:
Conduct a Courthouse
Name Search

This will be just like checking a name against a sex offender registry. If you're lucky, you'll be able to do this over the phone with a cooperative court clerk. If not, you'll have to go in person to the courthouse or mail in a request for information. If no cases are found under the name you are investigating, you won't need step three. If the name you are checking on is found, you'll need to review the court file.

Step Three:
Review Court Files

You'll need to review the court file for two reasons. The first is to make sure you've got the right person, even though the names match. You'll be using personal identifiers you have for the person you are investigating to compare with those found in the court file. Secondly, after you've made a positive identification through the personal identifiers, you'll want to read through the file to see what crimes the person was charged with and ultimately convicted of.

Plan B:
Hire a Private Investigator

After having a brief taste of what will be involved in conducting a criminal court check, are you hesitant to move forward? If you want the information, but don't want to burn the shoe leather, there's another option — simply hire a private investigator to do a criminal background check for you. Call him or her up, briefly explain what you need done and ask for a quote. Depending on the area of the country, this might cost you anywhere from $100 to $200. See page 76 for suggestions on where to find a P.I.

Now, if you're a do-it-yourselfer, the following sections will give you a more detailed look at each of the three steps in doing a criminal court check.

217

The Details of Conducting
A Criminal Court Search

Finding the right courthouse to check in is easy if you know what city or county to search in. Obviously, the goal here is to search in the areas where the person being investigated is believed to have previously lived. This task becomes more difficult if you don't have this information.

Let's take the easy path first. This is when you have information that the person you are investigating has lived in one area for most of his adult life. Obviously, this is where you'll want to search criminal court records.

You'll remember in the chapter "Obtaining Personal Identifiers", I spoke of using courthouse records to develop personal identifiers on a given person. We'll follow much the same procedure here. To refresh your memory, most areas divide their criminal courts into two main sections. The upper, or superior court, is for felonies. The lower, or municipal court, is for misdemeanors. (Note: The names of these courts vary from state to state. In some areas the upper courts may be known as Circuit, District or Supreme Court. Lower courts may be known as District or County courts.)

You should start by calling directory assistance and asking for the phone number for the criminal court in the area you are concerned with. Your primary focus should be on the superior court, or the court that handles felony cases.

Once you've been provided with a phone number, go ahead and call it to get things started. When you call the courthouse, your key question will be, "Is this the court that handles felonies for my town?" If you're told that the number you are calling is for misdemeanors or traffic matters, don't hang up! Instead, ask the clerk for a phone number for the court that does handle felonies.

By now, you should be armed with the right phone number for the right courthouse. If the person you are investigating has lived in more than one county, then you'll need to repeat the process for each area you want checked. An experienced P.I. could deftly handle this in minutes, but it may take you longer.

Now let's take a less easy example. What if you want to do a background check on someone who's currently living in your town, but previously lived elsewhere? Obviously, the trick here will be to find out where the person previously lived. Here are some things to try:

• If you know or are acquainted with the subject of the investigation, you may already have the answer to this. He may have told you where he was from before moving to your area, conveniently omitting the fact that he had a stopover in state prison on the way to your town. Or, perhaps you're a landlord. apartment manager or employer and have access to an application form in which prior address information was divulged.

• A person's Social Security Number can also be a tip-off as to the person's prior state of residence. The first three numbers of a person's Social Security Number are actually a code that tells what state the person resided in at the time of issuance. If you have the person's SSN, say from some type of application form, then you'll at least have an idea of whether he or she is native to your state. (A chart showing the SSN state-of-issuance codes can be found in the "Resource Kit" at the back of this book.)

• Look for signage on the person's car or truck which may provide clues as to prior place of residence. Often a person's car indicates all sorts of personal information — usually a lot more than most people would realize. This might be a license plate holder naming the dealership and city where the car was purchased. There might be a sticker for a sports team or a parking decal for an employer, school or apartment complex.

• Finally, if you still haven't been successful, you can always hire a private investigator to determine a person's prior places of residence. In the biz, we refer to this as an "address history". This should normally be a fairly simple matter and will cost $100 to $200. Tell the P.I. you're doing a background check to determine if a person is a previously convicted sex offender and you need to know his prior addresses. For any P.I. worth his salt, this should be a piece of cake. The P.I. will research DMV, credit card, and other databases and come back with some information for you soon.

By this point, you should have obtained some information about where the subject of your investigation formerly lived. This could have been through his own admissions, word of mouth, public records or by hiring a private investigator for assistance. You're now ready to contact the courthouse to learn if they have any cases on file for a person with the same name as the person you are investigating.

In review, the process will follow these steps:

• You'll call directory assistance and obtain the phone number for the criminal court that handles felonies in the jurisdiction(s) where the person you are investigating lives or has lived.

• You'll call the court and see if the clerk will conduct a name search for cases over the phone. Some courts offer this service and some don't. If you're lucky and this is one of those courts, you'll get your answer right then and there. If the court won't do phone searches, you'll have to go down to the courthouse in person, or make a mail-in request. Mail-in requests should be regarded as a last resort because the courts are slow in responding and requests are often lost.

• If you've done a name search at the court (by phone, in person or by mail) and no cases come up under the name of the person you are investigating, you can wind down your investigations here.

• If you've done a name search at the court and cases come up under the name you are checking, be sure to ask for the file numbers, filing dates, and charges. If cases are found, you're ready for the third and final step.

• You'll be visiting the criminal court to review cases that come up under the name of the person you are investigating. First, you'll need to review the files to see if the person named has the same personal identifiers as the person your are investigating. More often than not, this will entail comparing the full legal name and date of birth of the person you are investigating with those of the person named in the criminal court file.

• After a positive identification has been made, you'll then want to roll up your sleeves and read through the file. You'll find out all sorts of goodies, including what crime the person was charged with and convicted of. Make sure you also take a good look at other material in the file such as probation reports and transcripts — these may tell whether or not the person has had other run-ins with the law as well.

The Federal
Prison Check

Now, there's one more government source that merits a word or two — although it will be fairly unusual for you to find information of value here.

I've already told you about statewide criminal checks and criminal court checks. Both of these are part of either local or state criminal justice systems. There is also a federal criminal system. This consists of courts and prisons for persons who have broken federal laws.

It is fairly rare for sex-related offenses to be tried in the federal system. The federal system focuses mainly on tax cheaters, drug traffickers and interstate fraud matters. However, sometimes sex-related offenses will be tried in the federal court system. Typically, these will be cases where state lines have been crossed, such as in the case of a child abduction. Cases where sexually explicit material of children has been transmitted via the Internet or the U.S. mail would also be tried in the federal system.

Persons who have been convicted in the federal system and have been sent to a federal prison can be identified via Bureau of Prison records. This information is open to the public and includes the names of all persons who have been incarcerated in a federal prison since 1981. Previously, the information was just a phone call away. However, effective May 1, 1999 the information became available only by filing a Freedom of Information Act (FOIA) request.

Making a FOIA request is easy. Send a letter or fax and mark it "FOIA Request". Include words to the effect of "I am requesting the federal prison incarceration history of Joe Sample whose date of birth is.....under the Freedom of Information Act." Be sure to include your mailing address as all results are returned by mail.

Mail your FOIA request to *Federal Bureau of Prisons, Attn.: FOIA Office, 320 N. First Street, N.W., HOLC Building - Room 738, Washington, D.C. 20534.* Or, your request can be faxed to *202-307-0828*. There's also an online request form, called e-FOIA. Go to *www.bop.gov*, then click on the FOIA button. (Note: Results from requests made by fax or over the Internet are still returned by U.S. mail.) Your FOIA request is a free service offered by the Bureau of Prisons and the results should be returned to you within three weeks.

UNREGISTERED SEX OFFENDERS:
NAME SEARCHES

Here's an overview of the steps needed to conduct a name search to determine if a person is an unregistered sex offender. (Community searches for unregistered sex offenders are not possible.)

STEP ONE:

43 out of 50 states make statewide criminal checks available to the public. Check the *Guide to Statewide Criminal Checks* to learn what's available in your state. If available, conduct a statewide criminal check on the person you are investigating. However, be aware that the criminal history of offenders who were incarcerated in other states will not be detected by this method. If your state does not offer statewide criminal histories, proceed to step two.

STEP TWO:

Contact criminal courts where the person being investigated has previously lived to determine any past criminal cases. Review any cases found. If two or more personal identifiers are matched, a positive identification has been made. If less than two personal identifiers are matched, a positive identification has not been made. If you do not have personal identifiers for the person you are investigating, see chapter, "Obtaining Personal Identifiers."

WARNING SIGNS

WARNING SIGNS

Are there warning signs that a particular person may be a child molester or some other type of sex offender? Perhaps by the way the person speaks, acts or looks? Or where he congregates? How about by his marital history or sexual orientation? The answer to these questions is *sometimes yes, sometimes no.*

The single greatest warning sign that a particular person might be a danger to those around him is a prior criminal conviction for violent or sexual offenses. Clearly, if you have knowledge that a particular person has been previously convicted of a violent crime or certain sex offenses, vigilance is in order.

But what about less obvious warning signs for situations where a person does not have a known criminal history? Perhaps this might be a relative, a neighbor or a camp counselor.

Warning Signs:
The Child Molester

There are two basic subgroups of child molesters. Those in the first group, "pedophiles", are distinguished by the fact that they are sexually attracted to children. Those in the second group, often called "situational child molesters", are not sexually attracted to children. Rather, they act out of a variety of motives. Included in

WARNING!

The warning signs described in this chapter do not necessarily mean that sexual assault has occurred or will occur. Further, absence of the warning signs in this chapter are NOT a guarantee that sexual assault will not occur. These "warning signs" are for informational purposes only.

this group might be, for example, a socially retarded or generally abusive person who sees children as easy targets. Pedophiles will tend to have many more victims throughout their lifetime — sometimes *hundreds*. The situational child molester will tend to have far fewer victims and sometimes the molestation will be a once-in-a-lifetime event.

Not surprisingly, the pedophile child molester is easier to identify through warning signs. He is driven by a sexual compulsion that often dictates certain recognizable behaviors. On the other hand, the situational child molester is much more difficult to identify due to the haphazard nature of his motives and actions.

• *In nine out of ten child molestations, the child molester is known by his victim. The molester may be a family member, stepfather, coach or other respected adult figure.*

• *Three out of four molestations occur in either the home of the child or the home of the molester.*

• *The pedophile molester may show a keen interest in children and may situate himself in close proximity to them by volunteering with youth organizations or by otherwise frequenting places where children can be found. The pedophile may be seen by other adults as having a special gift in his ability to communicate with and be liked by children.*

• *The pedophile may seek out single mothers as a ploy to gain access to their children.*

• *Photography may be a hobby of the pedophile. He may take non-sexual photographs of children in public places. Later, he may take sexually explicit photographs of his victims both for his own gratification and for use in blackmailing his victims into silence.*

• The pedophile may attempt to "court" his next victim by showering him or her with gifts, money or attention. Later, the gifts and attention are withheld from the child until he or she submits to the molester's advances.

• The pedophile molester may seek to lower his victim's inhibitions by assisting the child in changing his or her clothes, by "sleepovers" and by showing sexually explicit material. Anytime a child reports being intentionally shown sexually explicit material by an adult, this should be considered a possible precursor to actual physical molestation.

• The pedophile will often have been a victim of child molestation himself.

• The pedophile will invariably be a collector of sexually explicit photographs of children. In addition, he may be in possession of news articles, books or legal information about child molestation. There are several organizations that support the pedophile belief system. If a person is found to be in possession of the brochures or other materials of one of these organizations, great caution should be exercised.

Warning Signs:
The Child Victim

Children who have been sexually abused may harbor the abuse as a secret out of fear or embarrassment. There are many warning signs that a child may have been victimized. Here are some of the most important ones:

• *Dramatic, unexplained changes in the child's behavior ranging from sudden aggressiveness to withdrawal. Excessive crying and fear of specific people or places should also be noted.*

• *In younger children, bed-wetting, nightmares and fear of being left alone are warning signs. Regression to infantile behavior, such as thumb-sucking, should be noted. A sudden interest in sexual matters is a further warning sign. This could be manifested as talk about sex organs that is beyond the child's current stage of development. Attempts by the child to fondle him or herself, or peers is another warning sign. Any unexplained genital injury or venereal disease is, of course, an obvious warning sign that must be investigated further.*

233

• In teenagers, warning signs can include drug and alcohol abuse, depression, delinquency and suicidal thoughts and actions.

Warning Signs:
Sex Offenders
Who Target Adults

For the purposes of this section, the term sex offender is meant to describe the victimizer who targets adult, usually female, victims. Identifying this predator through behavioral or other indicators is difficult at best.

Especially in cases of stranger-on-stranger attacks, pre-indicators occur only in the last minutes leading up to an attack. In these scenarios, training in self-defense is the best line of defense as it is then too late to take preventative measures. Here's a look at some possible pre-indicators of potential danger:

• A person who has been previously convicted of a violent or sexual offense should be considered a risk to re-offend.

• Two out of three rapes are committed by an assailant who is known to the victim.

234

• *A potential attacker may not be the disfigured monster who is portrayed so frequently on television. Rather, he may be charming, "nice" and of average or above-average looks. He may use his charm and niceness to gain the trust of a victim before attacking.*

• *Always be alerted by his refusal of your "no" — this is often the first boundary put up by a woman, and if it is ignored by a male pursuer, it could be an indicator that he will not respect other boundaries as well.*

• *Other behavioral indicators include expressing anger or hostility toward women in general and exhibiting jealous, possessive or controlling behavior.*

• *Use of drugs or alcohol by either the potential victim or potential attacker may increase the probability of an assault. In the first case, the attacker may sense his victim's inability to fend off his efforts. In the second, an intoxicated male may be less inhibited and more likely to act out his aggressive instincts. One study showed that 45% of rapists were under the influence of alcohol or drugs at the time of their attacks.*

SEXUAL
PREDATOR

Resource
Kit

Organizations That Can Help

The Megan Nicole Kanka Foundation
P.O. Box 9956
Trenton, NJ 08560
Telephone: 1-800-MEGAN-11 or 609-890-2201

The Megan Nicole Kanka Foundation supports national and state-level efforts to strengthen sex offender registration laws and educates the community, parents and children on related issues. The Foundation is currently supporting a new initiative to require background checks on all adult supervisors of youth organizations via the FBI. Founded by the parents of Megan Kanka, Maureen and Richard Kanka.

Jacob Wetterling Foundation
P.O. Box 639
St. Joseph, MN 56374
Telephone: 1-800-325-HOPE
Website: www.jwf.org

The Jacob Wetterling Foundation works on a national level on the issue of non-family abduction to gather and provide resources, educate, raise awareness and provide a response to victim families. Founded by the parents of abducted child Jacob Wetterling, Jerry and Patty Wetterling.

KlaasKids Foundation
P.O. Box 925
Sausalito, CA 94966
Telephone: 415-331-6867 FAX: 415-331-5633
Website: www.klaaskids.org

In October of 1993, 12-year-old Polly Klaas was abducted from her home in the small town of Petaluma, California. She was later found murdered. The KlaasKids Foundation is run by Polly's father, Marc Klaas, and focuses on parental awareness and child safety efforts, as well as laws to protect children from criminals who target them.

National Center for Missing & Exploited Children (NCMEC)
Charles B. Wang International Children's Building
699 Prince Street
Alexandria, Virginia, 22314-3175
Telephone 703-274-3900 FAX: 703-274-2220
24-hour Hotline 1-800-THE-LOST (1-800-843-5678)
Website: www.missingkids.org

The National Center for Missing & Exploited Children is dedicated to locating and recovering missing and abducted children, and to raising public awareness of ways to prevent child molestation and sexual exploitation. Sponsored in part by the U.S. Department of Justice, NCMEC is also instrumental in assisting and consulting with local, state and federal law enforcement agencies in missing children cases.

NCMEC Regional Offices:

Adam Walsh Children's Fund
9176 Alternate A1A, Suite 200
Lake Park, FL 33403-1445
Telephone: 561-863-7900 FAX: 561-863-3111

NCMEC/California
18111 Irvine Boulevard, Suite C
Tustin, CA 92780-3403
Telephone: 714-508-0150 FAX: 714-508-0154

NCMEC/Florida
9176 Alternate A1A, Suite 100
Lake Park, FL 33403-1445
Telephone: 561-848-1900 FAX: 561-848-0308

NCMEC/Kansas City
7701 State Line Road, Suite B
Kansas City, MO 64114
Telephone: 816-361-4554 FAX: 816-361-9414

NCMEC/New York
275 Lake Avenue
Rochester, NY 14608
Telephone: 716-242-0900 FAX: 716-242-0717

NCMEC/South Carolina
2008 Marion Street, Suite C
Columbia, SC 29201-2151
Telephone: 803-254-2326 FAX: 803-254-4299

Rape, Abuse and Incest National Network (RAINN)
635-B Pennsylvania Ave., SE
Washington, DC 20003
Telephone: 1-800-656-HOPE FAX: 202.544.3556
Website: www.rainn.org

The Rape, Abuse and Incest National Network (RAINN) is a non-profit organization that operates a toll-free hotline for victims of sexual assault. Operational 24 hours a day. Incoming calls are routed to the nearest of over 750 rape crisis centers nationwide. Founded by singer Tori Amos.

Childhelp USA National Headquarters
15757 N. 78th Street
Scottsdale, Arizona 85260
Telephone: 480-922-8212 FAX: 480-922-7061
National Child Abuse Hotline: 800-4-A-CHILD
Hearing impaired only: (TTY): 800-2-A-CHILD
Website: www.childhelpusa.org

Childhelp USA is dedicated to meeting the physical, emotional, educational, and spiritual needs of abused and neglected children, focusing efforts and resources upon treatment, prevention, and research. Child abuse can be reported at 800-4-A-CHILD.

Glossary of Terms

CERTAIN SEX OFFENSES - A general term which, for the purposes of this book, describes the collection of criminal offenses that would typically qualify an offender for registration under the Jacob Wetterling Act. These offenses include kidnapping of a minor (except by a parent); false imprisonment of a minor (except by a parent); criminal sexual conduct toward a minor; solicitation of a minor to engage in sexual conduct; use of a minor in a sexual performance; solicitation of a minor to practice prostitution; any conduct that by its nature is a sexual offense against a minor; rape, or sexual assault whether the victim is a minor or an adult. Typically *not* included are sex related offenses such as prostitution and indecent exposure.

CHILD MOLESTATION - Any illegal sexual contact, attempted contact or other activity with a minor. Some states have legal thresholds defining children as anyone under 16, 14 or 12 years of age.

CHILD MOLESTER - A general term used to describe any person who engages in illegal sexual activity with a child or children.

COMMUNITY SEARCH - A method of searching a sex offender registry to determine if there are any registered sex offenders living in a specific geographic area — usually city, county or zip code. Community searches are not available in all states.

CRIMINAL CHECK - An investigation to determine if a person has a prior history of criminal convictions. These are available to the public on a statewide basis in many states. In the states where statewide criminal checks are not available, criminal records are still available at the local level in criminal courts.

242

DEFENDANT - In criminal cases, the person who has been charged with a crime; in civil cases, the person who is being sued.

DOB - Slang for Date of Birth. Pronounced "Dee-Oh-Bee".

FEDERAL COURTS - Courts where crimes relating to violation of federal law are heard. Typical sex crime cases found here involve the crossing of state lines or illegal uses of the Internet or postal system for transmitting sexually explicit material.

INDEX - At a courthouse, the master list of names indicating persons who have cases on file. Usually stored on microfiche, microfilm or computer.

JACOB WETTERLING ACT - A federal law that mandates each state maintain a sex offender registry. It also sets standards for the registries. (See full text, page 251.)

MEGAN'S LAW - A widely used term that is often applied to any law which requires the notification of the community when a sex offender is present. There is a federal Megan's Law, as well as state versions in each of the fifty states. (See full text of the federal version, page 249.)

MUNICIPAL CRIMINAL COURTS - Criminal courts that handle misdemeanors (as opposed to felonies). In different parts of the country these may be referred to as District, County, Justice of the Peace or other names.

NAME SEARCH - A method of determining if a particular person is either a registered or unregistered sex offender. To determine if he is a *registered* sex offender, his name will.be checked against his state's sex offender registry as allowable under Megan's Law. To determine if he is an *unregistered* sex offender, his name will be checked against either state or local criminal records.

PAM LYCHNER ACT - The Pam Lychner Act led to the creation of a national sex offender database, which is maintained by the FBI. The national database is available to law enforcement agencies only. (See full text, page 258.)

PAROLE - The act of releasing a convicted person early from prison to serve out his time in the community under supervision.

PEDOPHILE - A person who is sexually attracted to children. If the pedophile does not act on his urges, he is not a child molester. Not all child molesters are pedophiles. If they do not have a sexual attraction to children, they are situational child molesters.

PERSONAL IDENTIFIERS - Any of several unique forms of personal information which further identify a person beyond his or her name. These include full legal name, date of birth, Social Security Number, photograph and address.

PROBATION - The conditional release of a person convicted of a crime into the community as an alternative to incarceration.

PUBLIC RECORD - Information that is lawfully available to any member of the public upon request. Typically this includes court files and many other government records.

RAPE - A sexual assault that includes forced intercourse.

RECIDIVISM - The tendency of an offender to commit new crimes after release from prison. Experts believe that sex offenders have a roughly 1 in 4 chance of being re-arrested or re-convicted for another sex-related crime.

REGISTERED SEX OFFENDER - A person who has been convicted of certain sexual offenses that require registration under the Jacob Wetterling Act as a sex offender in his state of residence. Under Megan's Law, the information may be releasable to the public, depending on the state in question.

SEXUAL ABUSE - A term generally applied to any sexual activity between a child and an adult or older child. It may occur over a long period of time.

SEXUAL ASSAULT - Any sexual contact between two people that is unwanted, forced, or otherwise not consented to.

SEX OFFENDER - Any person who has been previously convicted of any one of numerous sex-related crimes, including sexual assault, rape, child molestation and other crimes. Usually, convictions for prostitution or indecent exposure are not included unless a minor was involved.

SEXUAL PREDATOR - A term with slightly different definitions, depending on who is using it. Generally meant to describe a more serious category of sex offender who is habitual and/or violent by nature.

SEXUALLY VIOLENT PREDATOR - A legal description contained in the Jacob Wetterling Act and adopted by several states in their own version of Megan's Law. In the Wetterling Act, it is defined as "a person who has been convicted of a sexually violent offense and who suffers from a mental abnormality or personality disorder that makes the person likely to engage in predatory sexually violent offenses." Typically, a board of experts will make a determination as to whether or not a person should be designated as a sexually violent predator.

SITUATIONAL CHILD MOLESTER - A category of child molesters who are not sexually attracted to children, but rather, are motivated by other reasons, such as opportunity and moral indiscrimination.

SSN - Social Security Number. Always has nine digits in this configuration: XXX-XX-XXXX.

SUPERIOR COURTS - Upper courts that handle felony cases in criminal matters and major lawsuits in civil matters. Known by other names in various parts of the country, including Circuit, District or Supreme Court.

UNREGISTERED SEX OFFENDER - A person who has been arrested and convicted of a sex-related crime, but has not been required to officially register as a "registered sex offender" under Megan's Law in the state where he lives. Typically does not include convictions for prostitution or indecent exposure unless a minor is involved.

Social Security Number
State of Issuance Chart

001-003	New Hampshire
004-007	Maine
008-009	Vermont
010-034	Massachusetts
035-039	Rhode Island
040-049	Connecticut
050-134	New York
135-158	New Jersey
159-211	Pennsylvania
212-220	Maryland
221-222	Delaware
223-231	Virginia
232-236	West Virginia
232,237-246	North Carolina
247-251	South Carolina
252-260	Georgia
261-267	Florida
268-302	Ohio
303-317	Indiana
318-361	Illinois
362-386	Michigan
387-399	Wisconsin
400-407	Kentucky
408-415	Tennessee
416-424	Alabama
425-428	Mississippi
429-432	Arkansas
433-439	Louisiana
440-448	Oklahoma
449-467	Texas
468-477	Minnesota
478-485	Iowa
486-500	Missouri
501-502	North Dakota
503-504	South Dakota
505-508	Nebraska
509-515	Kansas
516-517	Montana

518-519	Idaho
520	Wyoming
521-524	Colorado
525,585	New Mexico
526-527	Arizona
528-529	Utah
530	Nevada
531-539	Washington
540-544	Oregon
545-573	California
574	Alaska
575-576	Hawaii
577-579	District of Columbia
580	Virgin Islands
581-584	Puerto Rico
586	Guam, American Samoa
587-588	Mississippi
589-595	Florida
596-599	Puerto Rico
600-601	Arizona
602-626	California
627-645	Texas
646-647	Utah
648-649	New Mexico
650-653	Colorado
654-658	South Carolina
659-699	Not Issued
700-729	Railroad Retirement Board
729-899	Not Issued

Note: There is also another tax payer identification number system called the *Tax Payer Identification System*. These numbers are also 9 digits and always start with a 9. They are issued by the Internal Revenue Service to foreign nationals who are not eligible for a Social Security Number, but have a federal tax liability.

Reprint of Federal Laws

Three federal statutes serve as the foundation of sex offender registration and community notification law in the United States. Although the media and others frequently refer to any or all of the laws as "Megan's Law", in fact Megan's Law is only one of the three laws.

Megan's Law requires states to release sex offender registration information "that is necessary to protect the public."

The Jacob Wetterling Act mandates that each state maintain a sex offender registry. It also sets standards for the registries.

The Pam Lychner Act mandates creation of a national sex offender database, to be maintained by the FBI. The national database is available to law enforcement agencies only and is scheduled to be fully operational by November 2000. The Act also requires the FBI to maintain sex offender registration and community notification in states unable to maintain "minimally sufficient" programs of their own.

Megan's Law

The first version of Megan's Law was passed in New Jersey. Ultimately, in 1996, a national version was passed as well. This is the national version:

SECTION 1. SHORT TITLE.

This Act may be cited as "Megan's Law".

SEC. 2. RELEASE OF INFORMATION AND CLARIFICATION OF PUBLIC NATURE OF INFORMATION.

Section 170101(d) of the Violent Crime Control and Law Enforcement Act of 1994 (42 U.S.C. 14071(d)) is amended to read as follows:

(d) Release of Information.--

(1) The information collected under a State registration program may be disclosed for any purpose permitted under the laws of the State.

(2) The designated State law enforcement agency and any local law enforcement agency authorized by the State agency shall release relevant information that is

necessary to protect the public concerning a specific person required to register under this section, except that the identity of a victim of an offense that requires registration under this section shall not be released.

Jacob Wetterling Act

On October 22, 1989, eleven-year-old Jacob Wetterling was returning home from a trip to a local convenience store in the small town of St. Joseph, Minnesota when he was abducted at gunpoint by a masked gunman. Jacob has not been heard from since and the crime remains unsolved. The boy's parents, Jerry and Patty Wetterling, were instrumental in the passage of the Jacob Wetterling Act — which requires each state to maintain a sex offender registry. Here's the full law:

TITLE XVII-CRIMES AGAINST CHILDREN

Subtitle A- Jacob Wetterling Crimes Against Children and Sexually Violent Offender Registration Act

SEC. 170101. ESTABLISHMENT OF PROGRAM.

(a) In General .-

(1) State guidelines .- The Attorney General shall establish guidelines for State programs that require-

(A) a person who is convicted of a criminal offense against a victim who is a minor or who is convicted of a sexually violent offense to register a current address with a designated State law enforcement agency for the time period specified in subparagraph (A) of subsection (b)(6); and

(B) a person who is a sexually violent predator to register a current address with a designated State law enforcement agency unless such requirement is terminated under subparagraph (B) of subsection (b)(6).

251

(2) Court determination .- A determination that a person is a sexually violent predator and a determination that a person is no longer a sexually violent predator shall be made by the sentencing court after receiving a report by a State board composed of experts in the field of the behavior and treatment of sexual offenders.

(3) Definitions .- For purposes of this section:

(A) The term "criminal offense against a victim who is a minor" means any criminal offense that consists of-

(i) kidnapping of a minor, except by a parent;

(ii) false imprisonment of a minor, except by a parent;

(iii) criminal sexual conduct toward a minor;

(iv) solicitation of a minor to engage in sexual conduct;

(v) use of a minor in a sexual performance;

(vi) solicitation of a minor to practice prostitution;

(vii) any conduct that by its nature is a sexual offense against a minor; or

(viii) an attempt to commit an offense described in any of clauses (i) through (vii), if the State-

(I) makes such an attempt a criminal offense; and

(II) chooses to include such an offense in those which are criminal offenses against a victim who is a minor for the purposes of this section. For purposes of this subparagraph conduct which is criminal only because of the age of the victim shall not be considered a criminal offense if the perpetrator is 18 years of age or younger.

(B) The term "sexually violent offense" means any criminal offense that consists of aggravated sexual abuse or sexual abuse (as described in sections 2241 and 2242 of title 18, United States Code, or as described in the State criminal code) or an offense that has as its elements engaging in physical contact with another person with intent to commit aggravated sexual abuse or sexual abuse (as described in such sections of title 18, United States Code, or as described in the State criminal code).

(C) The term "sexually violent predator" means a person who has been convicted of a sexually violent offense and who suffers from a mental abnormality or personality disorder that makes the person likely to engage in predatory sexually violent offenses.

(D) The term "mental abnormality" means a congenital or acquired condition of a person that affects the emotional or volitional capacity of the person in a manner that predisposes that person to the commission of criminal sexual acts to a degree that makes the person a menace to the health and safety of other persons.

(E) The term "predatory" means an act directed at a stranger, or a person with whom a relationship has been established or promoted for the primary purpose of victimization.

(b) Registration Requirement Upon Release, Parole, Supervised Release, or Probation .- An approved State registration program established under this section shall contain the following elements:

(1) Duty of state prison official or court .-

(A) If a person who is required to register under this section is released from prison, or placed on parole, supervised release, or probation, a State prison officer, or in the case of probation, the court, shall-

(i) inform the person of the duty to register and obtain the information required for such registration;

(ii) inform the person that if the person changes residence address, the person shall give the new address to a designated State law enforcement agency in writing within 10 days;

(iii) inform the person that if the person changes residence to another State, the person shall register the new address with the law enforcement agency with whom the person last registered, and the person is also required to register with a designated law enforcement agency in the new State not later than 10 days after establishing residence in the new State, if the new State has a registration requirement;

(iv) obtain fingerprints and a photograph of the person if these have not already been obtained in connection with the offense that triggers registration; and

(v) require the person to read and sign a form stating that the duty of the person to register under this section has been explained.

(B) In addition to the requirements of subparagraph (A), for a person required to register under subparagraph (B) of subsection (a)(1), the State prison officer or the court, as the case may be, shall obtain the name of the person, identifying factors, anticipated future residence, offense history, and documentation of any treatment received for the mental abnormality or personality disorder of the person.

(2) Transfer of information to state and the FBI .-

The officer, or in the case of a person placed on probation, the court, shall, within 3 days after receipt of information described in paragraph (1), forward it to a designated State law enforcement agency. The State law enforcement agency shall immediately enter the information into the appropriate State law enforcement record system and notify the appropriate law enforcement agency having jurisdiction where the person expects to reside. The State law enforcement agency shall also immediately transmit the conviction data and fingerprints to the Federal Bureau of Investigation.

(3) Verification .-

(A) For a person required to register under subparagraph (A) of subsection (a)(1), on each anniversary of the person's initial registration date during the period in which the person is required to register under this section the following applies:

(i) The designated State law enforcement agency shall mail a nonforwardable verification form to the last reported address of the person.

(ii) The person shall mail the verification form to the designated

State law enforcement agency within 10 days after receipt of the form.

(iii) The verification form shall be signed by the person, and state that the person still resides at the address last reported to the designated State law enforcement agency.

(iv) If the person fails to mail the verification form to the designated State law enforcement agency within 10 days after receipt of the form, the person shall be in violation of this section unless the person proves that the person has not changed the residence address.

(B) The provisions of subparagraph (A) shall be applied to a person required to register under subparagraph (B) of subsection (a)(1), except that such person must verify the registration every 90 days after the date of the initial release or commencement of parole.

(4) Notification of local law enforcement agencies of changes in address .-

A change of address by a person required to register under this section reported to the designated State law enforcement agency shall be immediately reported to the appropriate law enforcement agency having jurisdiction where the person is residing. The designated law enforcement agency shall, if the person changes residence to another State, notify the law enforcement agency with which the person must register in the new State, if the new State has a registration requirement.

(5) Registration for change of address to another state .-

A person who has been convicted of an offense which requires registration under this section shall register the new address with a designated law enforcement agency in another State to which the person moves not later than 10 days after such person establishes residence in the new State, if the new State has a registration requirement.

(6) Length of registration .-

(A) A person required to register under subparagraph (A) of

subsection (a)(1) shall continue to comply with this section until 10 years have elapsed since the person was released from prison, placed on parole, supervised release, or probation.

(B) The requirement of a person to register under subparagraph (B) of subsection (a)(1) shall terminate upon a determination, made in accordance with paragraph (2) of subsection (a), that the person no longer suffers from a mental abnormality or personality disorder that would make the person likely to engage in a predatory sexually violent offense.

(c) Penalty .-

A person required to register under a State program established pursuant to this section who knowingly fails to so register and keep such registration current shall be subject to criminal penalties in any State in which the person has so failed.

(d) Release of Information .-

The information collected under a State registration program shall be treated as private data except that-

(1) such information may be disclosed to law enforcement agencies for law enforcement purposes;

(2) such information may be disclosed to government agencies conducting confidential background checks; and

(3) the designated State law enforcement agency and any local law enforcement agency authorized by the State agency may release relevant information that is necessary to protect the public concerning a specific person required to register under this section, except that the identity of a victim of an offense that requires registration under this section shall not be released.

(e) Immunity for Good Faith Conduct .-

Law enforcement agencies, employees of law enforcement agencies, and State officials shall be immune from liability for good faith conduct under this section.

(f) Compliance .-

(1) Compliance date .-

Subject to paragraph (2), each State shall have not more than 3 years from the date of enactment of this Act in which to implement this section, except that the Attorney General may grant an additional 2 years to a State that is making good faith efforts to implement this section.

(2) Ineligibility for funds .-

(A) A State that fails to implement the program as described in this section shall not receive [*H8839] 10 percent of the funds that would otherwise be allocated to the State under section 506 of the Omnibus Crime Control and Safe Streets Act of 1968 (42 U.S.C. 3765).

(B) Reallocation of funds .-

Any funds that are not allocated for failure to comply with this section shall be reallocated to States that comply with this section.

Pam Lychner Act

Pam Lychner was a Houston, Texas-area real estate agent when she was attacked in a vacant house by a twice convicted felon. Fortunately, Lychner's husband arrived at the scene and intervened. The Lychners successfully lobbied for the passage of the law which bears her name. In essence, the law mandates the creation of a national sex offender registry, to be maintained by the FBI. The national sex offender registry is available to law enforcement only. Here's the full law:

SECTION 1. SHORT TITLE.

This Act may be cited as the "Pam Lychner Sexual Offender Tracking and Identification Act of 1996".

SEC. 2. OFFENDER REGISTRATION.

(a) Establishment of FBI Database.--

Subtitle A of title XVII of the Violent Crime Control and Law Enforcement Act of 1994 (42 U.S.C. 14071) is amended by adding at the end the following new section:

SEC. 170102. FBI DATABASE.

(a) Definitions.--For purposes of this section--

(1) the term 'FBI' means the Federal Bureau of Investigation; (2) the terms 'criminal offense against a victim who is a minor', 'sexually violent offense', 'sexually violent predator', 'mental abnormality', and 'predatory' have the same meanings as in section 170101(a)(3); and (3) the term 'minimally sufficient sexual offender registration program' means any State sexual offender regis-

258

tration program that--

(A) requires the registration of each offender who is convicted of an offense described in subparagraph (A) or (B) of section 170101(a)(1);

(B) requires that all information gathered under such program be transmitted to the FBI in accordance with subsection (g) of this section;

(C) meets the requirements for verification under section 170101(b)(3); and

(D) requires that each person who is required to register under subparagraph (A) shall do so for a period of not less than 10 years beginning on the date that such person was released from prison or placed on parole, supervised release, or probation.

(b) Establishment.--

The Attorney General shall establish a national database at the Federal Bureau of Investigation to track the whereabouts and movement of--

(1) each person who has been convicted of a criminal offense against a victim who is a minor;

(2) each person who has been convicted of a sexually violent offense; and

(3) each person who is a sexually violent predator.

(c) Registration Requirement.--

Each person described in subsection (b) who resides in a State that has not established a minimally sufficient sexual offender registration program shall register a current address, fingerprints of that person, and a current photograph of that person with the FBI for inclusion in the database established under subsection (b) for the time period specified under subsection (d).

(d) Length of Registration.--

A person described in subsection (b) who is required to register under subsection (c) shall, except during ensuing periods of incarceration, continue to comply with this section--

(1) until 10 years after the date on which the person was released from prison or placed on parole, supervised release, or probation; or

(2) for the life of the person, if that person--

(A) has 2 or more convictions for an offense described in subsection (b);

(B) has been convicted of aggravated sexual abuse, as defined in section 2241 of title 18, United States Code, or in a comparable provision of State law; or

(C) has been determined to be a sexually violent predator.

(e) Verification.--

(1) Persons convicted of an offense against a minor or a sexually violent offense.--

In the case of a person required to register under subsection (c), the FBI shall, during the period in which the person is required to register under subsection (d), verify the person's address in accordance with guidelines that shall be promulgated by the Attorney General. Such guidelines shall ensure that address verification is accomplished with respect to these individuals and shall require the submission of fingerprints and photographs of the individual.

(2) Sexually violent predators.--

Paragraph (1) shall apply to a person described in subsection (b)(3), except that such person must verify the registration once every 90 days after the date of the initial release or commencement of parole of that person.

(f) Community Notification.--

260

(1) In general.--

Subject to paragraph (2), the FBI may release relevant information concerning a person required to register under subsection (c) that is necessary to protect the public.

(2) Identity of victim.--

In no case shall the FBI release the identity of any victim of an offense that requires registration by the offender with the FBI.

(g) Notification of FBI of Changes in Residence.--

(1) Establishment of new residence.--For purposes of this section, a person shall be deemed to have established a new residence during any period in which that person resides for not less than 10 days.

(2) Persons required to register with the FBI.--Each establishment of a new residence, including the initial establishment of a residence immediately following release from prison, or placement on parole, supervised release, or probation, by a person required to register under subsection (c) shall be reported to the FBI not later than 10 days after that person establishes a new residence.

(3) Individual registration requirement.--

A person required to register under subsection (c) or under a minimally sufficient offender registration program, including a program established under section 170101, who changes address to a State other than the State in which the person resided at the time of the immediately preceding registration shall, not later than 10 days after that person establishes a new residence, register a current address, fingerprints, and photograph of that person, for inclusion in the appropriate database, with--(A) the FBI; and (B) the State in which the new residence is established.

(4) State registration requirement.--

Any time any State agency in a State with a minimally sufficient sexual offender registration program, including a program established under section 170101, is notified of a change of address by a person required to register under such program within or outside of such State, the State shall notify--

(A) the law enforcement officials of the jurisdiction to which, and the jurisdiction from which, the person has relocated; and (B) the FBI.

(5) Verification.--

(A) Notification of local law enforcement officials.--The FBI shall ensure that State and local law enforcement officials of the jurisdiction from which, and the State and local law enforcement officials of the jurisdiction to which, a person required to register under subsection (c) relocates are notified of the new residence of such person.

(B) Notification of FBI.--

A State agency receiving notification under this subsection shall notify the FBI of the new residence of the offender.

(C) Verification.--

(i) State agencies.--

If a State agency cannot verify the address of or locate a person required to register with a minimally sufficient sexual offender registration program, including a program established under section 170101, the State shall immediately notify the FBI.

(ii) FBI.--

If the FBI cannot verify the address of or locate a person required to register under subsection (c) or if the FBI receives notification from a State under clause (i), the FBI shall--

(I) classify the person as being in violation of the registration requirements of the national database; and

(II) add the name of the person to the National Crime Information Center wanted person file and create a wanted persons record:

Provided, That an arrest warrant which meets the requirements for entry into the file is issued in connection with the violation.

(h) Fingerprints.--

(1) FBI registration.--
For each person required to register under subsection (c), fingerprints shall be obtained and verified by the FBI or a local law enforcement official pursuant to regulations issued by the Attorney General.

(2) State registration systems.--

In a State that has a minimally sufficient sexual offender registration program, including a program established under section 170101, fingerprints required to be registered with the FBI under this section shall be obtained and verified in accordance with State requirements. The State agency responsible for registration shall ensure that the fingerprints and all other information required to be registered is registered with the FBI.

(i) Penalty.--

A person required to register under paragraph (1), (2), or (3) of subsection (g) who knowingly fails to comply with this section shall--

(1) in the case of a first offense-- (A) if the person has been convicted of 1 offense described in subsection (b), be fined not more than $100,000; or (B) if the person has been convicted of more than 1 offense described in subsection (b), be imprisoned for up to 1 year and fined not more than $100,000; or

(2) in the case of a second or subsequent offense, be imprisoned for up to 10 years and fined not more than $100,000.

(j) Release of Information.--

The information collected by the FBI under this section shall be disclosed by the FBI--

(1) to Federal, State, and local criminal justice agencies for--

(A) law enforcement purposes; and

(B) community notification in accordance with section 170101(d)(3); and (2) to Federal, State, and local governmental agencies responsible for conducting employment-related background checks under section 3 of the National Child Protection Act of 1993 (42 U.S.C. 5119a).

(k) Notification Upon Release.--

Any State not having established a program described in section 170102(a)(3) must--

(1) upon release from prison, or placement on parole, supervised release, or probation, notify each offender who is convicted of an offense described in subparagraph (A) or (B) of section 170101(a)(1) of their duty to register with the FBI; and (2) notify the FBI of the release of each offender who is convicted of an offense described in subparagraph (A) or (B) of section 170101(a)(1).

SEC. 3. DURATION OF STATE REGISTRATION REQUIRE-MENT.

Section 170101(b)(6) of the Violent Crime Control and Law Enforcement Act of 1994 (42 U.S.C. 14071(b)(6)) is amended to read as follows:

(6) Length of registration.--

A person required to register under subsection (a)(1) shall continue to comply with this section, except during ensuing periods of incarceration, until--

(A) 10 years have elapsed since the person was released from prison or placed on parole, supervised release, or probation; or

(B) for the life of that person if that person--

(i) has 1 or more prior convictions for an offense described in subsection (a)(1)(A); or

264

(ii) has been convicted of an aggravated offense described in subsection (a)(1)(A); or

(iii) has been determined to be a sexually violent predator pursuant to subsection (a)(2).

SEC. 4. STATE BOARDS.

Section 170101(a)(2) of the Violent Crime Control and Law Enforcement Act of 1994 (42 U.S.C. 14071(a)(2)) is amended by inserting before the period at the end the following: ", victim rights advocates, and representatives from law enforcement agencies".

SEC. 5. FINGERPRINTS.

Section 170101 of the Violent Crime Control and Law Enforcement Act of 1994 (42 U.S.C. 14071) is amended by adding at the end the following new subsection:

(g) Fingerprints.--

Each requirement to register under this section shall be deemed to also require the submission of a set of fingerprints of the person required to register, obtained in accordance with regulations prescribed by the Attorney General under section 170102(h).

SEC. 6. VERIFICATION.

Section 170101(b)(3)(A)(iii) of the Violent Crime Control and Law Enforcement Act of 1994 (42 U.S.C. 14071(b)(3)(A)(iii)) is amended by adding at the end the following: "The person shall include with the verification form, fingerprints and a photograph of that person.".

SEC. 7. REGISTRATION INFORMATION.

Section 170101(b)(2) of the Violent Crime Control and Law Enforcement Act of 1994 (42 U.S.C. 14071(b)(2)) is amended to read as follows:

(2) Transfer of information to state and the FBI.--The officer, or in the case of a person placed on probation, the court, shall, within 3

days after receipt of information described in paragraph (1), forward it to a designated State law enforcement agency. The State law enforcement agency shall immediately enter the information into the appropriate State law enforcement record system and notify the appropriate law enforcement agency having jurisdiction where the person expects to reside. The State law enforcement agency shall also immediately transmit all information described in paragraph (1) to the Federal Bureau of Investigation for inclusion in the FBI database described in section 170102.

SEC. 8. IMMUNITY FOR GOOD FAITH CONDUCT.

State and Federal law enforcement agencies, employees of State and Federal law enforcement agencies, and State and Federal officials shall be immune from liability for good faith conduct under section 170102.

SEC. 9. REGULATIONS.

Not later than 1 year after the date of enactment of this Act, the Attorney General shall issue regulations to carry out this Act and the amendments made by this Act.

SEC. 10. EFFECTIVE DATE.

(a) In General.--

This Act and the amendments made by this Act shall become effective 1 year after the date of enactment of this Act.

(b) Compliance by States.--

Each State shall implement the amendments made by sections 3, 4, 5, 6, and 7 of this Act not later than 3 years after the date of enactment of this Act, except that the Attorney General may grant an additional 2 years to a State that is making good faith efforts to implement such amendments.

(c) Ineligibility for Funds.--

(1) A State that fails to implement the program as described in

266

sections 3, 4, 5, 6, and 7 of this Act shall not receive 10 percent of the funds that would otherwise be allocated to the State under section 506 of the Omnibus Crime Control and Safe Streets Act of 1968 (42 U.S.C. 3756).

(2) Any funds that are not allocated for failure to comply with section 3, 4, 5, 6, or 7 of this Act shall be reallocated to States that comply with these sections.

SEC. 11. SEVERABILITY.

If any provision of this Act, an amendment made by this Act, or the application of such provision or amendment to any person or circumstance is held to be unconstitutional, the remainder of this Act, the amendments made by this Act, and the application of the provisions of such to any person or circumstance shall not be affected thereby.

267

WANTED:
Your True Story

The author of this book is interested in your true story! Did you use *Sexual Predator* to identify a registered or unregistered sex offender? If so, what were the circumstances and outcome of your efforts?

All replies will be treated confidentially. Please send your story via e-mail or U.S. mail.

By e-mail, send to:

research@crimetime.com

By U.S. Mail, send to:

SP True Stories
c/o Crime Time Publishing Co.
PMB 224
289 S. Robertson Blvd.
Beverly Hills, CA 90211

SEXUAL
PRE DATOR

Re-Order Information

Order on the Internet direct from the publisher using your credit card for fast delivery at *www.crimetime. com.*

Also available at many leading booksellers.

To order by mail, send $14.95 plus $3.50 S&H by check, money order or cashier's check to **Crime Time Publishing Co., 289 S. Robertson Blvd., PMB 224, Beverly Hills, CA 90211**. Sorry, credit cards not accepted on mail orders. (California residents must add 8.25% sales tax — $1.23.)

WWW.CRIMEtIME.COM

Books.
Software.
Information.
Updates.
24/7.

WWW.CRIMEtIME.COM